AS TO POLO

By William Cameron Forbes

Revised and updated by Sukey Forbes

mother
chukker

PUBLISHING

For Joan + Laura!
See you on The field!

Sukey

All rights reserved.

Published by Mother Chukker Polo Publishing

ISBN: 978-0-9980446-0-6

EDITOR'S NOTE

The original author of this book, my great-great uncle William Cameron Forbes "Cam" has always loomed large in my life. Having grown up in the same house in which he lived, my entire life has been steeped in anecdotes and memorabilia from his extraordinary time spent around the world for work and leisure.

Long before I took up polo I remember walking through the polo field where he would play with friends on our property and imagining the cast of characters who would come through and play a friendly match in the first half of the 1900s. It is a long and gently sloping field surrounded by the ocean on one end and forests on the other three. The field has long since become an open pasture for grazing cattle or a quiet spot for a gentle gallop during a trail ride. The cast of characters with whom he played reads like a who's who in turn of the century polo, seasoned with some big surprises like Rudyard Kipling and General George Patton.

Though I'd always been fascinated with the old polo mallets, trophies and gear that were on display on the walls throughout my childhood home, I never had the opportunity to learn to play until my adult life. One afternoon in northern California after a hack ride with a friend around her polo property I was introduced to the polo instructor arriving for the summer season. Within half an hour I had signed up for a lesson and that first lesson sparked a curiosity in me to learn about every aspect of the game. Stepping in lightly is difficult in polo, not least because proper polo requires a string (minimum of 4) of ponies requiring daily exercise, training, love and care on top of the constant honing of one's mental and physical skills. Consider it a bit like playing chess, on horseback, at top speed, while also swinging a long stick at a small ball. Then add in a linebacker trying to tackle you and your horse from the side and perhaps a truer picture might begin to emerge of the variables on the field. In polo, both horse and rider need to be in split second sync with each other as well as their other 3 teammates—7 if you count the horses.

In trying to learn a bit about the game I read numerous books on the polo history, field position and technique but was most impressed by Cam's short guide in *As To Polo*. Though originally published in 1911 the material is largely still salient. It became clear that the book—with a few updates for language and changes in the game—should be back in circulation. In that vein, I have taken it upon myself to edit and update *As To Polo* for the new millennium.

Much of the language is more formal and in keeping with the time period and standards of the early 1900s, I have kept most of it and edited out the more egregious parts that I found unpalatable (particularly as a woman) to digest. Polo was an all-male sport up until the 1970s and my Uncle Cam was well rooted in the ways of Boston Old School. I do wonder how he would feel about women playing the sport side by side on teams as equals with men in this new wonderful era of the sport. Women were allowed to join the US Polo Association in the 1970s, and now represent 40% of its membership and the largest growing demographic of players. Prior to that time, legendary female players such as Sue Sally Hale would put on wigs and fake facial hair in order to join the men on the field. Her daughter, Sunny Hale, brought women into the highest ranks in polo when she was offered a spot playing in the US Open in 2000. Her team won that year.

With regard to gender, I have gently tried to insert the feminine into the text by keeping much of the player pronouns as male but referring to the horses as female. Both sexes are well represented now on the field and yet, for the flow of the text, I did not want to be confusing by switching back and forth with pronouns.

There are areas of the book that are either beyond my learning polo brain and/or parts with which I do not wholly agree. In a few cases, I have edited them out without ill effect to the book. In others, I have left them in; and in a few other cases, I have weighed in as "editor" for a comment or two.

I do hope you will enjoy this updated version of *As To Polo* as both a time stamp on polo at the turn of the last century, and also as a timeless primer for the basics on polo. I have made every effort to remain true enough to the nature of William Cameron Forbes as has been passed through my family in stories, photographs, and other archival material. It is my belief that he would be proud to have this book he wrote back into the polo circulation.

Sukey Forbes 2018

INTRODUCTION

In fourteen years' experience as a polo player I have seen many players of several years' experience who had elementary faults that ought to have been eliminated in the first few weeks of their instruction. This has impelled me to write down some points on polo drawn from observation and from the instruction I have been privileged to receive. It is hoped that these may prove useful to others.

I began polo under exceptionally favorable auspices in a growing club, the first team of which played few outside matches and devoted its principal energies to the home practice games, so that polo was nearly continuous and the practice little broken up by match playing.

The first team was not composed of brilliant players and had depended for its success upon skill and team play. The four members had played several years together and each one used his head, thought out beforehand the proper strategy of each play, and kept winning matches because the handicap committee could not bring itself, in view of the fact that the merits of the individual players were by no means superlative, to give them greater handicaps than were carried by their more brilliant brethren who had lost to them through lack of coordination of the team parts.

In my second year of polo the No. 2 on this team stopped playing for a while, and in my third year I made his position on the team and, as a result, got into many matches and had the advantage of having three trained men, who had played together for years, holding their posts and keeping me to mine. Credit for this good team play and consequent success was wholly due to the admirable captaincy of that noble sportsman, Samuel Dennis Warren, of Boston.

It is much easier to start right than to unlearn a fault to which one has become habituated. If before beginning to play, the player learns to start the stroke from the perpendicular, for example, and to bring his mallet up to the perpendicular again, making one complete circle, he will avoid an error most pernicious in its results, which mars the play of a number of players—that is, carrying the stick at any angle or starting the stroke with the head of the mallet near the ground which, while not always fatal, is inimical to good hitting. It seems a pity that any player should ever begin polo without learning how to hold his mallet.

These notes have been very hastily thrown together, without much regard for form, and I have purposely left many repetitions in the text. The same thing will be found to be said over and over again, sometimes under one head and sometimes under another. This has been done with a view to emphasizing the more important things and showing that they are important, not only as a matter of individual play, if found under that heading, but also as a matter of team play, if found there, or as a detail in the matter of hitting or horsemanship, if found under the chapters dealing with those subjects.

Many of the suggestions herein contained are things which I have personally found useful, but I cannot tell whether or not they are accepted by the best players. Where these things are matters of personal development, and such as not learned from masters of polo or found in their books, I have adopted the device of saying "I am accustomed" to do this or that. I do this to avoid laying down the law or using the didactic form of saying that these things should be done thus or so. It is possible that some players who have had difficulties may find that some of these methods will help them. If I am wrong, and if players know better ways of accomplishing these things, I present my apologies.

I am not in any way offering this book as a guide to players who have already achieved high rank, because I have never myself held a high rating as a polo player, nor could I hold my own in really fast play. I believe, however, that these suggestions will enable beginners and players who have not had the opportunity of playing on or against very well-trained teams to avoid many of the faults to which beginners are liable and to put themselves in position so that when they have passed the earlier stages they will have less to unlearn and be in position to advance very much more rapidly under worthier instructors.

This book is written in the hope that it will prove useful to polo.

W. C. F.

TABLE OF CONTENTS

CHAPTER ONE

THE GAME

Polo is a most difficult game to learn. There are three cardinal things, each of which must be so learned as to be nearly habitual before the player can hope for excellence. The first of these is horsemanship; the second, hitting; the third, the strategy of team play. There are many variables that come into the game: there is the personal equation of the men; and there are the characteristics of the different sorts of horses belonging to the different players, each horse having its direct effect upon the play. The attention of the player must sometimes be directed to his horse, sometimes to his individual play, and sometimes to the teamwork. He should strive to make a reasonable excellence in all three of these so nearly habitual as to be able to direct his attention upon one which is presenting usual difficulties without letting the others go entirely by the board.

Where ten or eleven men are banded together to play polo on certain afternoons of the week it is necessary for everyone to be present in order to make up a game. Polo enthusiasts should refuse to allow their business or pleasure to interfere with polo afternoons. They should make these sacred to polo. It is not fair to the other payers who are maintaining ponies and expecting a game to have them lose their day of sport because one of the players happens to want to do something else for the afternoon.

The saddling and getting ready the horses, the fixed day, the fact that polo is in the neighborhood and that people will drive for long distances to see the practice in the afternoon make polo practices such an event as is the practice of no other game. The assurance of regularity in taking exercise is very advantageous to busy men and women whose work may be so absorbing and the demands on whose time may be so exacting as to cause them continually to neglect to fulfill engagements for other games more easily put off, as golf, tennis, or other sports, where it is more easy to fill up numbers in case of delinquencies. For a busy individual, directing large enterprises, I recommend polo as the surest way of keeping in trim.

It is true that polo is a dangerous game. It is however, much more dangerous for beginners than for experts, and I see no necessity for players doing reckless riding, nor is there any possible excuse for foul riding. The first care of every player should be to make the game absolutely safe by avoiding committing fouls, which are usually, *per se*, dangerous riding.

After watching a number of inexperienced men and women trying to play polo, I prepared a number of suggestions—or one might almost say axioms—for polo, which I wish that every beginner could be compelled to commit to memory before taking one's place on the polo field.

These are as follows:

IT IS BAD POLO

1. To take the ball round the field except when saving goal

2. To knock out or over.

3. To hit long strokes toward the sides in the offensive half of the field or hit into the offensive corners.

4. To try for goal from too great a distance or from too sharp an angle. Play approach shots.

5. For two of one side to ride for the ball at the same time. This is an inexcusable blunder.

6. For two of one side to ride out the same opponent

7. For two of one side to gallop parallel to each other. Either one or both are inexcusably out of place.

8. For any player to keep his pony galloping parallel to the ball.

9. To support your own man from too close.

10. To let your corresponding opponent when in position, ride clear (FIG 25)

11. To carry your stick anywhere but in the perpendicular

12. To back the ball into a rush of oncoming ponies

13. To hit the ball across when a back-shot will do.

14. To call "Go on" when you mean "Leave it."

15. To ride across the line of play too close to oncoming opponents.

16. To knock in directly in front of goal

17. To play for your opponent's misses

18. To leave an opponent whom you have covered to get to the ball when it was last hit by one of your side who is clear behind you.

19. To hit to an opponent who is clear.

20. To play in circles. Play up and down instead.

21. To try to do the work for another player of your side who is in position, in the belief that you can do it better.

IT IS GOOD POLO

1. To turn your horse to the new direction before reaching the ball if it is going slow or standing still, and if you have time.

2. To call "Turn" or some equivalent if you back the ball or miss it and it changes direction

3. To call "Go on" if you take the ball along

4. To hustle your corresponding opponent even if you can't reach him

5. To reach out and try to hook your opponent's mallet when he is hitting, even if it looks as though you couldn't reach it.

6. When on the right of way and headed to goal, to put on the greatest possible speed at the earliest possible moment.

7. To know where your corresponding opponent is all the time, and play so as to cover him.

8. To hit short strokes and play for a second chance when there is an opponent in front who is clear.

9. To maneuver to place yourself on the mallet or right side of your corresponding opponent.

10. To say the same thing always in the same way in calling to your side.

11. To make the line of play straight up and down the field except when defending goal.

12. To use your voice constantly to tell your own side what is going on.

13. To look where you are sending the ball before hitting and avoid putting it within reach of an uncovered opponent.

14. Always to wear a helmet to protect the head and face from getting hit by mallet and ball.

15. Not to leave your position except when taking out an opponent

16. To let the ball roll over your back line, if it will, when hit by an opponent.

17. To watch the eyes of your corresponding opponent and maneuver to cover or leave him when she is watching the ball.

IT IS BAD HORSEMANSHIP

1. To jerk your pony's mouth at the moment of hitting.
2. To stop the pony by turning her. Pull her up and turn her afterwards, otherwise you ruin your play and her legs.
3. To hit the pony with the mallet.
4. To gallop when a chance comes to pull up and wait.
5. To use a sharper bit or more harness than a horse absolutely needs.
6. To hold yourself in the saddle with the reins.
7. To ride into the line of play at a dangerous angle.
8. To turn to get into the line of play from too close to a pony that is riding straight. The ponies may trip.

IT IS GOOD HORSEMANSHIP

1. To use the voice before the rein, and both sparingly.

2. To sit well back in the saddle and let the horse do the hustling.

3. To bring the horse up almost to a standstill before turning her when the direction of the play is reversed.

4. To save your pony's head from being struck by opponent's stick by fending with your mallet.

5. To save your pony in every possible way. Don't gallop an unnecessary inch.

6. To stop your horse by the alternating system of pull and go, never by steady pulling.

Pertinent generalities:

1. An opponent's stroke spoiled is as good as a stroke made.

2. Match play is the best school for polo.

3. In case of doubt-

    No. 1 should ride to his man

    No. 2 should ride for the ball

    No. 3 should ride for the goal he is defending.

4. If you find yourself with nothing to do, maneuver to cover your corresponding opponent.

5. Anticipation of the movement of the play is the essence of success in polo.

6. Maneuver so as to keep the ball in sight at the moment it is struck.

7. Begin the stroke at the perpendicular and complete the full circle with one even swing.

8. In every play know where the corresponding opponent is, and remember that if you are not together, either one or both of you are out of place. In case of doubt, assume it is yourself.

9. To find position count the men ahead of you.

    If there are two more opponents than of your side ride hard to catch up with the further one.

    If there is one more opponent ride to him.

If there are equal numbers, ride the man beside or behind.

If there are more of your side, pull up and let one or two opponents, as the case may be, pass you.

These rules do not apply if you are on the ball or if the others are far out of position.

10. Don't lean out of the saddle when anyone whose mallet may reach you is swinging at the ball in your neighborhood. The mallet usually swings up and down. If you sit straight the pony will protect you from below, the helmet from above.

11. Don't ride fast toward the side and go over the boards at speed; pull up if possible.

12. Use the mallet and arm to fend against the possible blow of an opponent's stick whipping in from the side.

13. Whether in position or not, the man nearest the ball must take it rather than let it go to the other side.

14. In first-rate polo the ball will be traveling up and down the field at a maximum and around and across the field at a minimum.

15. Remember that opponents may easily be near enough to crook a forward stroke, when a back stroke can be made without interference. The back stroke is safest for defense.

16. Watch and make sure that you always strike the ball with the center of the mallet head.

17. The secret of hitting far is beginning the stroke soon enough on the forward strokes and late enough on the back strokes. Added distance will be given in all strokes by sharp use of the wrist.

18. The secret of team play is to cover your own position so thoroughly that any adversity will be the fault of the other man.

19. Good players will try to hit always to one of their own side, not to themselves.

20. In good teams no one cares who hits the goals.

21. Read the rules at least once a year.

CHAPTER II

THE POLO CLUB

The polo club has to conform to local conditions, and it is impossible to lay down any rule as to general characteristics, as in some places the club is a country club in which polo is an incident, interesting only to a comparatively small portion of its members; in others, the polo features is the whole thing. I shall, however, outline what I consider the ideal combination. This is a small club, organized principally for the purposes of polo, with a rambling and rustic clubhouse, situated in the country within easy reach of a number of players, owners of property in the neighborhood, who have clubbed together for their polo and other sports. There should be just enough members from some neighboring city who are in the habit of coming out and living at or nearby the club during parts of the summer months to give a homelike feeling to the club and a club population, which it would not get were it to depend on people having neighboring estates and living when in the country at home. People from the city could thus keep their ponies at the club, which should have large stables. There should also be facilities for such other seasonable sports as the country affords. The Meadow Brook Club in Long Island, the Myopia Polo Club of Massachusetts, Greenwich Polo Club in Connecticut and the clubs of Wellington, Florida on the East Coast; Santa Barbara Polo Club, Empire and Eldorado in Indio on the West Coast; and Denver Polo Club in the Rocky Mountains are clubs that answer more or less accurately to this description.

It would be well for the club to have two fields, and I have always fancied the idea of having polo every day. Three days a week could be given to the players with more than three ponies and the desire for fast and furious play, and three days to one and two pony players, to encourage beginners and players of smaller strings, or those who like exercise and do not care for the strenuous work that comes from the fast play in anticipations of matches, thus encouraging polo from the cradle to the grave. In this way, when the first team was off playing matches, all players would be able, by coming on the odd days, to get polo; also if one happened to be away on one of their regular polo days he could make up by coming out with the other set of players and thus get his chance to play and not lose a day of exercise and sport.

Every Club should have a wooden horse set in the middle of a cage, with sides that slope in such a way that a ball thrown in will roll toward the horse and come to a stop within hitting reach of the mallet. These walls slope up on the sides and end in a net which catches the ball and throws it back upon the sloping floor. A player by sitting on this wooden horse can concentrate their attention upon the stroke, the direction, the swing and speed of hitting, and the part of the mallet head on which the ball strikes, without having to think of a lot of other matters which tend to distract the attention. In the Philippines those teams that used the wooden horse regularly came out much the best in the tournaments.

An important feature of a successful club is, however, the right sort of groom. Each player's property should be known by the groom, who will take personal interest in seeing that everything is in place. When arriving to dress for polo each player's outfit should be laid out, boots properly cleaned and properly tree-ed, spurs neatly clean and laid by the boots, white trousers, shirt, and belt, underclothes, and whip, gloves, wrist straps, helmet, etc., and selection of mallets on a rope or a rack. Those mallets which have twisted or weakened heads or are damaged in any other way should be laid on the floor below or stuck in a separate corner, so that by no chance will the player be misled, in his hurry, to take one of them.

On the players' return from play they will have a raging thirst; and no drink is more grateful than that which first quenches the thirst that one gets on the polo field. Electrolyte drinks and water should always be available for during play. A selection of post-game beverages in addition to the non-alcoholic selections such as wine, beer and champagne are also traditional for post-game wrap up meetings, celebrating wins or soothing losses.

I used to have players trained so that everything prepared for polo was just as a matter of course and without orders. All ponies fit for play were brought to the field, with their respective saddles and bridles. They arrived with a bunch of fifty or sixty ponies composing the strings of all the players, either just before or just after the drag containing the players themselves.

After polo we all sat down and had a polo dinner, which was not the least enjoyable part of the afternoon, the crowd breaking up early or late, as they liked. With many of the finest polo players hailing from Argentina their influence has also infused post-game activities. These dinners now are often in the form of an Asado, the traditional informal barbeque of sausages and meats slowly grilled over a low pit. The post-game asado tends to include all players families as well as grooms and guests of the event and are a wonderful way of building rapport amongst players as well as mending any arguments of the day that may have happened during the heat of play.

I think, whatever the club may be, there should be a committee to care for the interests of polo, to be known as the Polo Committee.

This committee would determine such matters as the date of beginning games and opening the season and closing it, and such other matters as they may not have delegated to the captain. While the Polo Committee would make ground rules, fix the hours of play, the terms upon which the field could be used, hours in which it could be practiced upon other than the hours of play, and all matters connected with polo memberships, it should in no way undertake to interfere with the captain in such matters as the selection of the team or the conduct of the play of the team in matches, or of any member in play, except in so far as the general rules of the club are concerned.

Under certain circumstances it may be desirable to have a polo membership to carry with it the privileges of the club during the polo season only, and it should not be perhaps so costly as a regular membership with polo privileges. The polo privileges, however, whether to polo or to regular members, should carry with them a charge, as each player should pay something for the upkeep of the field and the expense of maintaining the games. As a rule is it not customary to charge admission to polo games, hence the only source of revenue for maintaining the field comes from the general revenues of the club or from the pockets of the polo players. The expense would vary somewhat with the number of players, which either makes two fields necessary or increases correspondingly the cost of maintaining one. It is doubtful if a polo field can be maintained without a very substantial call upon the pockets of all the players, except in the instance of a very large country club near some important city where the membership is so large that the proportionate part paid by each member for such a thing as maintaining a polo field is inconsiderable.

CHAPTER III

FIELD, PONIES, AND EQUIPMENT

The field should be 300 by 150 or 160 (or 275 x 145 meters) which is the equivalent of 10 acres or 9 American football fields, and the immediate surface is the most important part. While it is preferable to have the field absolutely level, different parts of the field may slope slightly from side to side or from end to end, or from the center toward the ends, or vice versa, without spoiling the play, provided that the ball rolls comparatively true. By this I mean that the surface of the field should be smooth enough so that the ball will roll on smoothly and not with a series of bounces up and down. This can be accomplished only by having the right kind of turf and by constant care in putting back the torn pieces of turf, and by regular addition of sand for water drainage. A good field also requires fairly constant rolling.

The side boards should be of three-quarters or inch board, 10 inches high, supported by posts set into the ground on the outside of the field. Great care should be taken that these posts have beveled edges and no nails standing out which could catch a horse's leg and tear the skin as she goes against them.

Although not contained in the ordinary book on polo, I consider it eminently desirable that the side board should curve in toward the goal post at the ends. A plan which I have adopted in laying out polo fields is to cut off 75 feet from each side on the ends, beginning the curve 150 feet from the ends and curving in on an easy curve to the goal line. This makes the field 300 feet wide on the goal line, instead of 450. The space saved cheapens the cost of the field without in any way hurting the game.

There should be at least 80 feet clear back of the goal posts, and a back board 18 inches high, painted dark, so that the balls may be easily recovered when knocked over the back line. This back board should overlap the side boards a few feet, and the ends very properly be curved a little toward the field so as to stop balls sent through at an angle. The goal posts should be skeletons, made light so as not to damage a horse by reason of impact; padded rubber or some wickerwork covered with canvas is good. The bottom of the post should be a circle of board, which should stand upon a base of the same diameter, set into the ground 18 to 24 inches, the top of the base being immediately level with the surface of the ground; in this a hold should be bored. The goal post is held in place by means of a wooden pin, which is set into the sunken post and also includes the circle of board which forms the bottom of the goal post. This pin holds the goal post in place and prevents its falling over when touched or when blown by the wind, but the impact of a horse breaks the pin and the goal falls down. It can be set in place again by the insertion of a new pin. A supply of pins should always be on hand at the goal post for such contingencies.

It is well to have flags places at the sides of the field fifty feet from the goal line so that the player or referee can inform himself by sighting as to the limit of closeness the ball may be approached on the knock in.

A white line should be placed across the center of the field but need not reach from side to side. The man in charge of practice should see that the teams line up for the throw in at different times in different parts of the center line, otherwise one place will be unduly torn up. In fact, before matches it is well to have the ball thrown in for practice to one side of the center line, in order to leave the center line untorn for the time of need. It is also well to move the goal posts from time to time, setting them at different places, especially for the limbering-up practice before polo as they receive the hardest wear and tear when everybody is trying to make goals. Players are apt to be very inconsiderate, and having struck a goal, immediately endeavor to round it out by brilliantly pulling up their horses or vent their displeasure at having missed a goal by jerking them up almost directly in front of the post. Pulling the horse up in this way invariably tears up the field and players should make a rule to let the horses gallop in practice until over the back line, where they can pull up without damaging anything. Captains and officers in charge of the play should call the attention of the players to the occasional necessity of saving the field in this way.

The field should be sub-drained and watered, and the best results are obtained if a gang of men are ready after each day's practice to come immediately out on the field and repair the most noticeable scars where ponies have cut the turf.

On practice days the players themselves can help out, after goals, turning over with their mallets pieces of sod which have been torn up and pushing them back into place as the ride back to the center of the field. The longer roots are exposed to the air the less likely they are to take vigorous hold on their being replaced. The tradition of inviting spectators on to the field for a glass of sparkling wine and to help replace divots is both helpful for the second half of the match and beneficial for the overall state of the field.

I shall not undertake to go into the question of the selection of ponies at great length. I like to see ponies that are well coupled and keep their feet well under them, and personally I sacrifice speed to handiness, although I know some players who sacrifice everything to speed. I never begin on a pony that is hard-mouthed. I do not advise beginners to try to teach themselves and the pony to play at the same time. They can do much better if they take a trained pony and concentrate their attention on themselves. I know experienced players who have ruined a pony or two every year through inability to handle them properly, usually on account of hard hands. With these players polo ponies habitually go wrong, as only an occasional horse is found that they can manage. Careful players with light hands can get along with almost any horse.

Tails of the ponies should be braided then folded back on the braid and secured in that shortened position to avoid the tail getting in the way of a stroke; and there is no doubt that it does where one is taking a full stroke and turning on the ball at the same time.

A pony should never be played without bandages or some sort of boots on the forelegs. In Dedham we always played in bandages, and so skillful were the grooms that almost never did a bandage come loose. With less skill in placing the bandages they are apt to become a menace, as a bandage unrolling can throw a pony in such a way as to make it dangerous. The referee should always stop play instantly when they see a bandage beginning to become unrolled.

The danger of too much pressure on the tendons, by reason of straps around felt boots, can be obviated by having elastic or Velcro straps. Playing without stout felt boots or plenty of thickness of bandage over the tendons invites disaster. Sooner or later the mallet or ball will hit these tender parts in a way that will ruin the horse.

I always make a point of getting my ponies of the same height. I do not believe in changing heights. I think it hurts hitting. If one changes the length of the stick it changes the distance of the hand from the ground, which is unfortunate, as the eye becomes accustomed to a certain distance and a man hits better with the fewest possible variables. In purchasing a string of mounts I should therefore, wherever possible, select ponies of even height.

EQUIPMENT- Many believe the Texas saddle is the best for polo. I do not believe in any saddle where the feet are kept under one. One sits too low in the saddle and lacks the rise which one gets from the Texas saddle in order to turn and to get the near side forward stroke. The editor has had great success playing in a set of Argentine saddles and with accommodations in saddle pads has had no difficulty fitting the saddles to a variety of pony body types.

It is advisable to buy a complete new set of girths stirrup leathers, and bandages every year. Do not trust to old ones. Also the saddles should be thoroughly overhauled each year to make sure the padding has not got packed down and that the girth straps have not got old and untrustworthy. Polo is dangerous enough anyway without taking chances, and the wetting and drying of perspiration from horse and rider which the saddle gets three times a week in polo season is enough to rot the strongest sewing. The breaking of a girth or a stirrup leather may mean a loss of life, and it is an unjustifiable risk to take.

I use many varieties of bits of different grades, from a rubber snaffle, which always has a steel chain through the rubber to the Hanoverian Pelham, with the long bars for curb, which is the sharpest bit that I use. I never attempt to use a Mexican bit with a high port, but will discuss the use of bits under the title of "Horsemanship." A horse should have the easiest bit that he will play well under and as soon as a horse plays perfectly under a sharp bit he should be given one less sharp. The usual bit that the average horse comes to is a Straight Bar Pelham, with short curb bars, the bit itself being round and smooth and of steel. This can be eased, in cases of sore mouth, by a leather cover, and, if the lips chafe, by leather discs set next to the lips.

Crane believes that most ponies play much better with a port varying from one-half inch to two inches in height. I have never used ports.

Until the pony is entirely handy he should have a martingale. I have no use for a running martingale, as it disarranges the curb and snaffle in the hand, bringing the snaffle the lower of the two where it does not properly belong; and I have never seen that it helped. The standing martingale answers every purpose, and I believe it to be the best. As the pony improves in play the martingale should be lengthened gradually, and finally done away with entirely, on a good many horses, on the general rule that the less harness a horse is encumbered with the better.

Some horses have to have shoulder straps to hold the saddle forward, the peculiar shape of their barrel making it impossible to tighten the girths so that in the course of play the saddle won't slip back.

The personal polo outfit—The breeches should be white and made of twill or denim, which lasts well, holds its shape, and gives excellent protection to the legs. Spandex in the material can allow for a decent stretch. The boots should be brown, and made stiff all the way down, so as to protect the ankles from blows. Black boots should not be used, as they soil the clothes of everybody who comes in contact with them.

I never use a glove on my right or mallet hand, believing that I have better control of the stick with the bare hand. The editor is a big fan of gloves on both hands both for grip and sun protection. Soft washable gloves are available from many vendors.

A soft glove and tape on the handle save a tired forearm and prevent cramps. I have never used either, but have been troubled from time to time with cramps, and should recommend such equipment for those who need it.

On the left hand I wear a glove until the fingers are tough enough not to be blistered by action of the reins. Soft chamois gloves are the best. Some prefer white cloth gloves, and these are probably better in rainy weather, although as a rule one does not play polo when it rains. All players should make a rule to have one glove always at the field. By turning a glove inside out it can be used on the other hand.

Players should always wear polo helmets. To play without one is to play in immediate danger of loss of life or of an eye, and is an unjustifiable risk. These helmets should be made so that they protect face and eyes from the blows in front and against chance blows from the side. In 2019 the newest safety features will be part of the technology of a new style of helmet and as such starting in January of 2020 all players will be required to wear helmets conforming to the new technology.

I always carry both whip and spur on all ponies. I use spurs that stand out not more than a half inch or three-quarters of an inch from the heel, so that I have to reach for the pony in order to spur him. I recommend this for all but extremely tall players, as a precaution against spurring the horse unintentionally. I have found the most satisfactory whip to be a whip about 3 ½ or 4 feet long, a sharp cutting whip made very limber, with a horn button about two inches wide, flat on the side toward the hand. This whip, carried between the reins and the left hand, will almost never get away and does not need to be strapped to the hand. I drop one barely once a year. The length of the whip gives the advantage of being able to hit the pony without losing hold on the reins as the turn of the wrist while the hand is well forward will still reach his quarters.

The polo mallet can be conveniently described as being composed of three parts—the head, the handle, and the stick, the stick being that part to which the handle and the head are attached.

Sticks should be very carefully selected and carefully used. The principal thing to avoid is buying sticks which are whippy toward the handle. This is a most common defect, and I find it ruins any stick for me. Personally, I always use a good stiff stick, the total weight of the mallet being from 470 to 490 grams; however, the weight of the mallet is a good deal a matter of preference. In general I believe the back should have a heavy stick for distance, and No. 2 a light one for quickness. In purchasing mallets, care should be taken to get absolutely straight sticks and to see that the angle to the head to the stick is always the same. To measure this, a model can be marked somewhere on the wall and every stick verified so as to preclude the possibility of variations in this important particular.

It has been my experience that flat sides to the handle are far preferable to round handles. Flat sides parallel to the head enable one to tell by the feel of the handle when the mallet is swinging true, a distinct advantage, as the eyes are needed for watching the ball.

When a stick is secured that suits perfectly, it is a good plan to weigh it carefully and register the weight, and then balance it and register the point at which it balances. If in selecting new sticks care be used to approximate in nearly as possible the weight and balance of the stick that has proved to be the best, one variable element will be eliminated, or at least reduced to a minimum.

The place where a mallet begins to weaken first is usually that part of the stick just above where it is inserted into the head. The reason that the stick goes out at this point is that the ball when struck is likely either to be bouncing up so as to hit the stick just above the head, or perhaps the mallet is swinging a little bit low, bringing the round of the ball against the stick. These sticks are of malacca or bamboo, and have an outer shell which cracks in perpendicular slits. Once the shell has cracked the stick loses its strength and the head begins to twist. There are two ways of reinforcing the winding. The first one, and one which all players should insist on, is by reinforcing the stick at the point just above the head with a little strip of metal, preferably steel, curved so as to fit the curve of the stick and placed under the winding which is also used for the same purpose, namely protection of the stick at that point. Two such metal strips should be provided for each stick, one to catch the front strokes, the other to catch the back strokes. The strips should go about one fourth around the stick and should extend about 3 inches above the head. The other way of protecting the stick is to wind it with rubber bands or tape made for the purpose—from three to six at intervals around the stick over the winding and immediately above the head to catch the impact of the ball. Many players use both of these devices.

CHAPTER IV

HORSEMANSHIP

The management of the horse is a most important element in polo. A good horseman does not necessarily make a good player, but a man who is not a good horseman is very seriously handicapped in his effort to become a good polo player, very much as is a lame man in the matter of running races. The first thing to get is a seat. When I was a boy I made a point of coming in from my ride every day with my gripping muscles tired to the point of aching, and I recommend this practice to every horseman. It gives one an unconscious seat. When I began riding, I was told by my preceptor that a man should always turn his toes in so as never to give the appearance of rides with his toes pointed diagonally away from the horse. I gradually came to acquire this way of riding, and it was not to be accomplished by bending at the ankles in such way as to make the toes point forward, but it lay in the position of the muscles of the thigh. When a man takes a seat in the saddle he should move himself just a little forward to as to throw the fleshy muscles of the thigh outward and backward and place in direct contact with the saddle the inside of the leg from the knee bones up. Having placed himself thus, he will find that automatically his feet now hang so as to throw them directly forward, and that in order to get them out of this position it is necessary to turn the ankles in an awkward position outward or to let the upper part of his leg assume a different position in connection with the saddle and ride gripping with the back of the leg rather than the inside of it.

Having set himself in his seat, the player should next look to his stirrups, which, in my judgment, should be of medium length, short enough so that he can stand up entirely clear of the saddle and turn around, so that in making the near-side forward stroke his right shoulder may be about over the ball on the left-hand side of his horse.

He should endeavor to acquire a position sitting quietly, well back in the saddle, with the feet well forward, and letting the horse do the speeding. He should not habitually stand up or lean forward, but by sitting right down in the saddle eliminate the greatest number of possible variations in the distance from the hand to the ground when hitting.

My cousin Allan Forbes is of the opinion that men should hit leaning forward, as he considers in this way they get better direction and more distance to the stroke. There is no question but that when it is desired to hit the across in front of the pony it is necessary to lean forward; but I am a firm believer in having the seat pushed well back toward the after end of the saddle, and not varying the distance to the ground, as is done by leaning forward or standing up in the stirrups in making a stroke, excepting always for the near-side work, when it is necessary.

Avoid as much as possible, hitting under the pony's belly, as the stick or the ball is too likely to hit the pony's legs, and either of them may damage the pony.

The following remarks apply only to horses which have been thoroughly trained to the saddle and are well bitted. I do not undertake to give directions for the earlier instruction of a horse that has never learned the use of the bit. I have found that some who understand the training of horses have differed with my theories on the ground that beginning a horse with a sharp bit makes her afraid of it and that the best authorities recommend a light bit at first. To these I answer that I begin where they leave off; that my work is training a pony for polo and that I assume that one is already bridle-wise.

In training ponies, the most important thing is to get them interested in the game first and afterwards develop their speed. In training a pony I never let her get to speed until I have got her so much the master of the game that the desire for racing will not exclude the interest in the play.

The most important thing in handling a horse is the use of the reins. Many riders indulge in the practice, as pernicious in its results as to be almost wicked, of holding themselves in the seat with the reins. They seem to think that reins were given to them by a divine providence to steady themselves on the horse. When one considers that the mouth is one of the most tender parts of the horse's anatomy, and with well-trained horses the least touch can produce the desired result, it is nothing short of brutal to blunt this fine sense of the horse by misuse. New players should get horses to learn on that have extremely tender mouths and so little desire to run that they can be played with an absolutely loose rein. If they cannot get such a horse I should recommend putting on an extremely sharp bit, at least sharp enough so that the horse will not press against it and will stop instantly if the pressure is put on too sharply.

Having thus got a horse which can be ridden with a loose rein or by a series of the lightest kind of touches, they should then acquire their seat without ever holding on or assisting themselves in the seat by pressure on the reins. It is my positive belief that more good horses and more good polo ponies are ruined by this fearful habit of pulling than by all the rest of the causes put together. It takes two to pull, the rider and the horse. If the rider won't pull, the horse can't. I have known superb saddle horses that were almost unmanageable by men and which were mild as kittens with women. The reason was that they could not endure the hard hand of a man on the bit. Had they had a rider with sufficient skill to indicate to them by light touches, they would have been as docile as they were with women.

I have sometimes thought that an excellent way to learn how to press lightly on the rein would be to have the snaffle rein cut and tied together on each side by bits of string, which would break as soon as the pressure exceeded a certain reasonable amount, like a lightning arrester which fuses as soon as the current gets too strong. This would automatically prevent a rider from falling into the crazy habit of wrecking the horse's mouth, and yet this is what at least one-half of the players do when beginning, and a good many of them do through life. I have known players with whom all good polo ponies became pullers, and at the end of each year they found it necessary to buy new ones in order to keep themselves mounted. I attributed this tendency, in many instances, to the player's poor seat.

I have sometimes wondered why a little machine has not been invented for registering the pressure on the mouth of the horse by different riders. It surely would not be a difficult device to have the two parts of the rein entering a machine, connected by means of a spring to a dial which would register the exact maximum pressure exerted by the rider. If the cold, hard fact that such-and-such a horseman managed his horse with a pressure indicated by the number 3 was presented to another horseman who habitually came in with a registration of 7 or 9, he would begin to study the causes for this phenomenon and perhaps correct the worst fault which a horseman can have. To polo players especially would I recommend the study of this very vital part of horsemanship. I have never heard of any such device as this having been attempted, so that it is merely a suggestion and might prove in practice to have none of the value that I imagine it would.

The function of a rein is not physically to stop a horse, but to telegraph to her the desire of the rider. Horses should be trained so that the least touch will indicate to them what is wanted and to obey this lest indication as soon as they receive it. That the rein is a physical means of stopping the horse is about as much of a fallacy as that the bootstraps are an excellent way of raising oneself from the ground. One might as well adopt the equal and opposite fallacy that the stirrups were an advantageous means for pushing the horse ahead, as all force used in pulling on the reins is derived from pressure on the legs and feet in the saddle and stirrups, so that by completing the vicious circle you are exerting your force to push the horse ahead in order to stop her. The fact is, of course, that the horse wants an indication of the desire of the rider, and as the inertia of going is something she does not like to change, particularly if there is another horse going pretty fast right alongside of her, the signal to stop must sometimes be fairly forceful to make the horse obey it.

I hold my reins with the snaffle on either side of the first finger (next to the thumb) and the curb on either side of the third (ring) finger, thus having one rein outside of the first finger and one rein in between each of the four fingers. As the hand is held thumb down, it results that the two upper reins are the draw and the lower reins the curb. In order to hold them at the same tension I can place my thumb over the reins and by pressing and gripping the reins with the hands I get a good grip. With this arrangement one can very easily adjust the reins by gripping the four reins with the right hand, and by slipping the whole left hand forward one gets a closer grip near the neck. By catching the upper part of the reins the draw is shortened, by catching the lower as it hangs the curb is shortened. The draw rein should always have a buckle and the curb never, so that in reaching for the draw rein if you feel for the buckle or look down and pick it out and slip one finger of the right hand through that you can be sure of shortening the draw rein. If you look for the sewed end and slip a finger through that or catch it with the hand to pull on, you can be sure you are shortening the curb.

Upon taking the task of updating *As To Polo* the editor would like to add that there are several correct ways to hold the reins and the more readily used one in the USA currently is the hand held palm flat, facing down with draw reins on the left side of the fourth finger and first finger s and curb reins on either side of the third finger. In this position as well, one rein will be located between each of the four fingers. The difference between these two hand positions is in the first position described the hand is held such that the fingers are stacked on top of each other with the left draw rein on the outside of the first finger. In the second, the hand is held such that the fingers are side by side with the left draw rein on the outside of the fourth finger. In any of the ways of holding the reins, the draw reins should be slightly looser than the curb reins.

I have adopted the following general methods of signaling my horse which have served my purpose:

For ordinary play the hand is held low and about over the pommel of the saddle. The pony understands that riding with the hand low indicates slight changes of direction rather than a sharp turn or turnabout. When I want speed I throw my hand forward, giving loose rein and touching the pony on the neck low down. The whip, which is always carried in the left hand, as I have explained elsewhere, is about four feet long and limber. I use it on the shoulder for starting the pony and on the quarters for extending her. I use the spur for steadying her as she approaches the ball and for making her press over to ride against another pony and for getting her away when another pony is pressed up against her. I also use it to start a pony quickly. I never use the spur for speed. To stop the pony, instead of taking hold of the curb rein, I find infinitely more effective to raise the hand. This changes the angle of the pull. A pull on the draw rein, which should always be a light one, is merely to steady the horse at the speed at which she is going and to hold her on the ball.

The advantage of lifting the hand is that the pony can instantly see and instantly knows that it is desired to change the play and stop. Before putting any pressure on the curb the voice should always be used, but its effect should not be spoiled by an agonized "Hoh! Hoh! Hoh!" such as you often hear players galloping down the field addressing their ponies, who are not paying the slightest attention to it. Give one good sharp "Whoa!" and then a sharp lift on the curb, the body being thrown well back on the back part of the saddle, so as to put the weight on the quarters, not on the forelegs, and then loosen the rein up instantly in order to let the pony get her head free and stop if she will. If she fails to stop, a second sharp pull on the curb, loosening the rein immediately, should bring her to hand. The moment she has stopped the reins should be thrown immediately loose and the hand lowered.

There is nothing more wicked and pernicious in polo than turning in circles at speed, and yet how many players will do it! Ponies should be turned always by stopping them in their tracks and then starting them again on the new course. There are occasions in polo when the exigencies of the game require turning at speed, as in following the ball around, but these are so few, compared to the cases when ponies should stop and turn, and are more apt to occur in playing against poor players than against good, that all players should first train their ponies to stop and turn and afterwards use them for whatever turning in circles may be necessary, because the ability to stop and turn does not preclude the other, whereas a habit of turning around at speed will prevent a horse from being of any use for really good polo.

In turning the pony, when it is my desire that she turn very rapidly and fast, I always lay the rein on the upper part of the neck, so as to get it in an unaccustomed place. The rein is pressed against the lower part of the neck more or less continually, so that there is nothing particularly new to the horse in the feel of the rein at that point. It almost never touches the upper part of the neck, near the ears, and I have found that a pony will jump around, when she feels the rein up there, infinitely faster than she will when the rein is pressed at the base of the neck; in fact it makes the signal for quick turning a distinct one, as opposed to a shifting of direction. I am able to turn my best polo ponies almost on a loose rein, touching the mouth very, very lightly, and by shifting the rein on the neck they know instantly whether I am attempting to shift the direction slightly so as to get nearer the play or whether I want to bring them around to place them in position to go in an opposite direction.

A most important thing in polo is the care and saving of the horse. I have spoken elsewhere of using the mallet to protect the horse from getting hit by opponents. I should only, under the most important circumstances, hit the ball through under the pony's belly when going fast, for fear of hitting the horse's legs either with the stick or the ball.

A horse may be greatly saved by resting her in play. A great many players, particularly beginners, feel that they have to gallop all the time, that they are not playing if they are not galloping, and when the opportunity comes for a moment's rest, when the horse can stand still or be galloping slowly, they are still galloping madly about and getting themselves out of position. To save a horse properly, it is necessary to know exactly how to play to an opponent. If you place your pony in such relation to that of your corresponding opponent that he cannot get at the ball without passing you, and you are vigilant about watching him, you can very often save your pony and hold her with very little exertion on the part of man and horse so as absolutely to cover your opponent. Thus if a ball comes back you may be able to meet it or if it passes you will be ready to turn and, by hooking or hard riding, prevent your corresponding opponent from getting the ball, and thus entirely cover your position. The polo player should make a rule never to gallop one unnecessary foot.

The best players get in the line of the play, which is the line the ball is traveling, and, always watching where the corresponding opponent is, hold themselves ready to pick up the play with a rush when the time comes. As soon as it is necessary, in order to prevent the opposing player from getting by or getting the ball, they should get up speed and hold it while the rush lasts. If a chance comes to hit the ball the player should then put his pony at top speed and come right along the right of way, going at such speed that nobody will risk coming into it at any angle but a safe one.

Ponies that are saved in this way get to know when speed is wanted of them and will respond to the rider's signal in a way which ponies that are needlessly galloped about by their riders never do. A pony that is needlessly galloped is always looking for a chance to save herself, as otherwise if she goes constantly at top speed she will soon be played out. The pony that is saved by her rider is fresh and eager for a rush and all the time waiting for a signal to move.

In speaking of equipment, I mentioned the matter of bit, which is one of the most important elements of horsemanship, and one that seems to be least studied and understood by those who are accustomed to use horses. I know in my own case, although I had ridden from the age of four, I knew practically nothing about bits or the science of bitting when at the age of 24 I took up polo. I grade my bits as follows:

1. Rubble snaffle that has served for but one of the very many ponies I have played

2. Steel snaffle, broken. I have always preferred this with large and flat rings

3. Straight-bar Pelham. This bit I find most of my ponies come to play. I have them with four different lengths of curb bars giving different degrees of leverage on the curb chain. Ponies with very light mouths can be helped by covering the bit with leather

4. Bit and bridoon. I use these with two different lengths of curb bars, medium and long. Some ponies have to be used permanently with a bit of the severity, but I try to work the ponies gradually to an easier bit.

5. Gag snaffle without curb

6. Gag snaffle with curb

7. Hanoverian Pelham with and without steel rings which revolve on the bit and prevent the horse from getting a grip on it with his teeth. This is the severest bit I have ever used.

I am not sure but that a horse might be broken of a desire to pull by the use of the Mexican high port, but I advise against the use of a bit like that for playing.

When first putting ponies into polo I test them until I find a bit they are afraid of and that they won't under any circumstances take hold of. Playing them then with a very light rein and an easy pull, I get them to obey the voice and the indication of raising the hand which presages a pull on the curb. At the start I usually have the curb chain very tight, so that the pressure on the jaw comes very quickly. In her first stages of development I usually have the pony's head tied down fairly low with the standing martingale. As soon as the horse has responded to this bit in such a way as to make me feel confident that she understands the signals and will obey them without the necessity for punishment, I immediately make the bit easier. The first step in this process is loosening the links on the curb chain so the curb will not begin to press until it is pulled a little farther back and lengthening the martingale to give the head more freedom. The next process is to move up into the next easiest bit in the way I have mentioned, sometimes skipping one or two. Sometimes I pass from Hanoverian Pelham clear to the straight-bar Pelham with the long bar on the curb, sometimes merely to the bit and bridoon, and this process continues as long as the horse is naturally at home and going satisfactorily with the easier bit. As the horse gets more and more perfect in the game, the standing martingale may be lengthened until finally, in some good horses, it can be taken off.

Crane has found that the position of the bit in the mouth makes a great difference with his ponies; some play better if the bit is not too high. I play all of my ponies with the bit just easily reaching the corner of the mouth without pressing.

The straight-bar Pelham with 3 ½ to 4 inch curb bars I consider one with is usually the most satisfactory; most ponies will come to play well with it.

The first three bits on the list can be used only on ponies with the most delicate and tender mouths and unusually responsive to the bit. In my experience only one out of four or five good ponies have such mouths, and there is no need of paralyzing the pony's mouth even if you have a sharp bit. If the policy which I recommend is adopted, the indications may be given with a very light touch, and horses will get along perfectly well even with the sharpest and most cruel bits. I play with very loose rein and pull on the bit the least possible amount.

After the earlier stages of training and testing are past, it is inadvisable, however, to play a pony under a very sharp bit, relying upon a light hand not to use it. The pony with a light mouth will be afraid of a sharp bit the minute it is in her mouth, and many ponies refuse to gallop against a bit which they are afraid of. If one wants to get speed out of a pony with a light mouth, he should put on the lightest bit with which he can stop the pony, because in this way only can he get his highest efficiency. The gentle handling of a pony in stopping has a great deal to do with the speed which can be gotten out of her, and light-handed players are apt to be the fastest. As speed is the essential requisite for really first-class polo- enough said.

The ponies also get to understand the feel of the legs in the saddle and will respond to them in turning, but I will leave to the expert horse trainers the various uses of the legs, to indicate to the horse the desire to turn, hanging leads, etc. I have never made much of a study of this, and have let my horse learn about the pressure of the leg more unconsciously than otherwise. Of course, she does learn it, because a player shifts position in the saddle in order to bring the horse around.

When a pony that has been playing steadily well begins either to pull or to have some trick, it indicates that something is the matter, and instead of putting on a sharper bit the player should find out the reason for this change. Nine times out of ten, the rider will notice that the pony's legs are beginning to go, or that she has trouble with her teeth, which is most likely to be the case if the pony holds its head to one side. The first indications I have of a pony weakening in their forelegs is the fact that she begins to take hold of the bit when she has not done so before. This means that the pony doesn't want to stop and that she is afraid of it. The cure is to lay the pony up and either "blister" or "fire" her, or if these measures are not necessary give her a good rest. If the groom is careless and does not tell the player that the legs are beginning to bother or swell and show signs of weakness in the tendons, by sharpening the bit and keeping on playing, it is possible to ruin a first-rate pony that otherwise, by immediate care, would have played for years. I have played some of my ponies seven years, and Allan Forbes played one of his ponies in all of his matches for a period of ten years. He played the position of No. 1 and often played only two ponies in his very important matches. He was active and light and knew the art of saving his ponies.

There are a number of niceties about polo which it is well for players to learn. In the first place, almost all ponies, when beginning, are awkward about taking the boards. Players should have their ponies trained to run along the boards and jump them at speed, going over them at angles without swerving, which they very readily learn to do. If the ponies are not specially trained to this they are apt to trip on the boards some time and go down or shy at them and possibly shy into another pony going at speed, which might make a foul which would be perfectly avoidable by a little foresight.

In coming up on the ball before hitting, the hand should be held low and exerting a slight pressure on the pony's mouth, enough to steady her and show her that the rider is alert. The greatest care should be taken to give no jerk whatever nor any very great change of the hands or legs at the moment of hitting. A jerk on the rein or a jab of the spur will surely result in the horse giving some little check as the stroke is made which will be most disastrous to the accuracy of the stroke. Ponies are often spoiled in this way, and it is a fault which takes a long time to cure. The best way I have found to cure ponies of a defect of this kind is to get them out where there are a number of balls lying around and to swing all the time so that the mallet is continually moving. If one ball is passed over without hitting because the pony tried to shy, the next ball may be taken, but in any case the utmost care should be taken not to catch the pony either on the bit or with the spur or whip when the stroke is made.

If the pony has a practice of shying from the ball occasionally, it is well to touch her with the spur before she reaches it, making the stroke without any touch either of the curb or spur; but if she shies at the time of hitting, punish her afterwards by giving her a sharp dig with the spur, possibly a sharp stroke of the whip, and accompanied by a good active reminder on the curb, all as in the nature of punishment. The pony should be then set at the ball again and reminded once again with the spur before the times comes to hit, not as the stroke is made. If she still persists in shying, she should be carefully drilled to eliminate it, but I recommend strongly against digging with the spur at the moment the stroke is made.

It is well to hang a polo mallet in the stall with a new pony in order to accustom her to the sight and nearness of it.

I shall not make any extended comment on the subject of training horses. Anybody who wants to train their pony had better read that which has been written on the subject by masters of polo. There are a great many exercises at which ponies should be put, such as bending between posts, riding past other ponies going at speed, pushing against other ponies, and turning and following the ball, etc. I have little time to do it, and do not feel expert at it. What little training of ponies I have accomplished has been done by taking a mallet and going out and hitting a ball around until I could get the pony into the game and then playing her until she became good, only staying by those which showed sufficient aptitude for the game to play after this imperfect and casual method of development.

The only suggestions I should make are that the rider should always try to be quiet with the horse and very first with her. If she develops any particular trait, such as shying, checking, or objecting to near-side work, throwing her head when the ball is struck, swerving over the ball or on back strokes turning before the ball is struck, practically the whole time should be devoted to curing such defect or defects until they are eradicated. It is most important that the horse should feel that the game is a matter of course, that it is the easy and natural thing and that there is nothing unusually exciting or strange about it.

CHAPTER V

USE OF THE MALLET

In treating this subject, "use of the mallet," I shall take up first the subject of hitting and then the manner or carrying the stick and its uses in hooking.

Strokes may be divided into the following general classes:

1. The full stroke forward (on the off side), which can be divided into

    (a) The straight stroke or one which follows the line of the ball to send the ball straight ahead.

    (b) The cross stroke, which swings across the line of the ball; and

    (c) The cut stroke, or stroke in which the head of the mallet is held at an angle to the direction of the stroke, with the object of deflecting the ball.

2. The back stroke (on the off side), with the same subdivisions as in the full stroke forward.

3. The near-side stroke forward.

4. The near-side stroke backward.

5. The half stroke forward, which also is divisible into the general subdivisions (a), (b), and (c).

Three-fourths of the game lies in the ability to play the full stroke, forward and back, on the off or right hand side of the horse; one fourth lies in the ability to hit in all other ways, as near-side strokes, turning the ball, etc.

The player should concentrate, therefore, on learning the full stroke well, in the belief that with the full stroke well learned one can become a first-rate player. Without the full stroke properly learned one can never amount to anything as a polo player. Excellence in all other strokes will in no way compensate for the failure to know the full stroke thoroughly.

1. *The full stroke*—(a) The full stroke is started with the mallet in the right hand, with the upper and outer part of the head pointed back, the hand somewhat advances but not raised. The stroke is made by drawing the hand back without raising it, well behind, and then swinging the stick with an easy full sweep, the hand passing way to the full reach forward, carrying the stroke through and bringing the mallet to the perpendicular, where it is again stopped and held. The head of the mallet thus describes an elliptical circle. The hand does not change its level, except on the down swing, but passes from well forward to well back and forward again. This movement of the hand covers a distance of about three feet each way, so that the head of the mallet will travel along the ground, if the horse is standing still, a distance of about three feet, and the ball will be hit if it is anywhere in that distance. In the first of these three feet the mallet will be descending, and if the ball is encountered there the descending stroke will tend to drive it into the ground and no distance in the movement of the ball will result. In the second foot the mallet will be traveling absolutely true along the ground, but with a slight upward tendency toward the end and maximum efficiency of the stroke is obtained. In the third foot the mallet will be rising and will tend to lift the ball and send it into the air. This is sometimes a desirable thing, but usually it is not. The player should usually calculate to hit the ball in the last six inches of the second foot, above referred to, when the mallet is nearly parallel

to the ground, with a slight tendency upward. Beginners almost always hit too late and thus hit the ball, if at all, in the first section and get no distance. There is no necessity for any very great strength in the blow. The weight of the mallet head carried with the movement of the swing, plus any movement that the hose may have, is sufficient to send the ball a normal distance. Greater distance may be obtained by making a swifter swing, and sometimes it is well, by a quick twist of the wrist, to send the ball an unusual distance. The player should always remember, however, that the most important thing in hitting is to start the stroke *soon enough*, so that the mallet will not have any downward tendency when it reaches the ball. Many players begin their stroke at the ground, having to describe a full swing of the mallet before hitting the ball, the strain on the arm in raising the mallet to the perpendicular being a wholly unnecessary one which takes as much muscle as the whole stroke does. The absurdity of hitting this way is too obvious for argument. It necessitates a very much nicer calculation as to the time when the swing should begin. If the pony is going at full speed and the ball is standing still, for a proper full stroke the player should begin his swing when about twenty feet away from the ball, if he has his mallet up; if he has it down, he has to begin just twice as far away, or perhaps a little farther, as to lift the mallet is a slower affair than to swing down. The practice of beginning the stroke with the mallet in any other position than the perpendicular has not one intelligent argument to commend it. It is contrary to all rules of good sense and practice, and should be eliminated at the very beginning.

The player should keep their eye on the ball, as in all other games, until the stroke is complete. If he takes his eye off the ball, it is his own fault if he misses it. He should also make sure on what part of the mallet head he is hitting. He should always hit it on the exact point of the mallet where the stick passes through. If he hits constantly to the right or to the left of the place where the stick enters the head, he will hit constantly inaccurately, as the mallet tends to turn in the hand with the pressure of a stroke anywhere on the mallet head but the center, and such turning will tend to send the ball either to the right or to the left, according to the side of the center on which the stroke is made. So that the players who want to get accurate hitting should see that they are hitting the center of the ball with the center of their stick. This can only be accomplished by concentrating attention on it and watching vigilantly and keeping at it until hitting accurately becomes habitual.

In calculating the time to hit, one has to take into consideration that there are two kinds of strokes—one when the ball is standing still and the other when the ball is moving. When the ball is standing still, the only calculation needed is the speed of the pony, which one can regulate and which in good play should be made as fast as possible. If the speed is increasing, one has to calculate the acceleration. When the ball is moving, one has to calculate the movement of the ball and the movement of the horse. If the ball is traveling in the same direction as the horse, and in the direction it is desired to send it, the matter becomes an extremely simple one, and it is hard to make a poor stroke unless the ball bounces. Where the ball is traveling very fast and the pony traveling equally fast alongside of it, it does not matter much when you begin your stroke. If the ball bounces, the player is entirely excusable if he misses it entirely. If the bounce is not too high and the player has swung accurately, the ball may be caught on the bounce by the stick; but, even so, he probably will not hit the center of the ball, even though the stroke were accurate, and thus the ball will be deflected to one side.

Crane comments that "players should watch the bounce and try to hit the ball as it strikes the ground, although the best players take it in the air when they have to."

Some players are quick and adroit enough to bend the elbow suddenly as the ball bounces up, thus catching it. This is a very brilliant play; but steadiness is what counts, and a player can feel satisfied if he always gets his stroke except when the ball bounces, and a player should not feel bad at missing it when he struck at the strategic and proper moment.

(b) and (c) I now come to the question of hitting the ball at an angle to the course in which it is traveling. There are two ways of changing the course of the ball—the cut stroke, made by swinging in the line the ball is traveling but with the mallet head held at an angle so as to turn the ball when it strikes, and the cross stroke, made by swinging across the line that the ball is taking. The merit of a cut stroke, as compared with that of a cross stroke, varies directly with the rapidity of the movement of the ball past the pony. If the ball is going past rapidly, the cut stroke is much safer; if going past very slowly or moving at the same rate, the cross stroke is better. The cut stroke is necessary when turning the ball away from the pony; turning toward the pony the cross stroke sometimes has advantages. The cut stroke requires the mallet to be centered more accurately on the ball because the angle at which the head is held presents a narrower surface with which to make the stroke that if the head were held square, as it is in the cross stroke. The difficulty of timing the cross stroke when the ball is moving rapidly past the pony is so much greater than the cut stroke that it much more than balances the disadvantage of the narrower surface of the mallet head in the former and renders the cross stroke so much more difficult to accomplish that the chances are all in favor of the cut stroke. It is probably that most players use a combination of the two, swinging somewhat across the line and giving an additional deflection to the ball by holding the mallet head at an angle. I believe this to be advisable and perhaps necessary when the ball is to be cut well across.

The experiments I have made indicate that the effective distance that the mallet passes along the ground---about two feet—is increased by about a foot by the movement of the pony when going at speed. In the back stroke the effective distance of the stroke is reduced by about six inches by the adverse movement of the pony. The accuracy necessary to place the mallet in contact with the ball throughout the distance of two fee, as in the cut stroke, is very much less than that necessary to hit the ball where the distance of possible contact is a matter of a few inches, as in the cross stroke. This difference is accentuated when the ball is moving toward the player, when the chance of hitting it squarely when the mallet is traveling along the line of the ball is in the ratio of something like ten to one over the chance of hitting it with a cross stroke. The cut stroke also has an advantage where the ball is being turned across the pony in that the mallet is not so likely to hit her as it is when swinging toward her.

Another point to be noted is that the cross stroke will send the ball a very much greater distance than the cut stroke. It is obvious that if the mallet head is held square, perpendicular to the direction that it is intended to send the ball a much greater distance than the cut stroke. It is obvious that if the mallet head is held square, perpendicular to the direction it is intended to send the ball, a much greater distance will ensue than if the ball encounters only that resistance which comes from a slanting or glancing blow with the mallet head held obliquely to the direction of the stroke. This, however, is not necessarily an argument in favor of the cross stroke, as direction is often infinitely more importance than distance, and especially in turning the ball a short stroke is usually more to be desired than a long one

Summing up, then, where the ball is passing the pony in either direction and it is desired to turn the ball away from the pony, the cut stroke is usually the only possible one; and when it is desired to turn the ball across the pony, it is much the safer stroke to try, as the cross stroke has to be calculated with great nicety, judging the speed of the horse, the speed of the ball, and the angle at which it will strike—all of which make a great many variables to be discounted. In the cut stroke, where the mallet is sent along the line in which the ball is traveling, the variables are reduced to a minimum, and there remains only the question of getting the proper angle and centering the sticks so that the mallet will meet the ball. The various ways of hitting, however, are subject to so many variations of circumstances that it is almost impossible to lay down rules. If the ball is traveling in the same direction as the pony, and at the same speed, it is very easy to hit it at any angle, for one can make the same stroke as one can with the horse and ball standing still.

When it is desired to turn the ball across under the pony's neck it is well to ride a little closer to the ball and lean forward, hitting the ball before you get to it. The more you wish to turn the ball the closer you will ride to it and the farther forward you will lean. Until at right angles the pony should be turned directly toward the ball and the stroke should be made under her neck. In this case, however, care should be taken not to swing too fiercely, as, with a reasonably whippy stick, the head may come right around and strike the player in the face, particularly if the ball is missed. Sometimes, when the angle is not too great, the ball can be made to clear the pony by bringing the pony up very wide, say, three or four feet from the ball, leaning well out of the saddle and turning the ball across in front of the pony. In any case care should be taken not to hit the pony with the stick or the ball, an event undesirable both from the point of view of possible injury to the pony and of spoiling the stroke.

Sometimes, where it is necessary to cut the ball across and no great distance is needed, it is well to chop at the ball, hitting in such a way that the mallet head will stop on the ground. This prevents tangling the stick with the pony's legs and often serves the necessary end.

In turning the ball away from the pony it will be found effective also to bring her up well to the side of the ball and then to hit a half stroke rather late. If a full stroke is attempted under these circumstances the mallet will often catch in the pony's tail, as the player will have it swing, rudder like, toward the side he is turning, and to get the stroke away one swings across from behind the horse. A half stroke will send the ball a nice distance to turn and reach.

2. *The back stroke*—In making the back stroke on the off (or right side), I always put my thumb down the center of the flat part of the handle and swing with much more rapidity than I do on the fore stroke, for the reason that the momentum of the horse is against the stroke, instead of being with it, and therefore much more force is needed to get distance.

In the forward stroke, most beginners hit too late. In the back-stroke they are almost certain to hit too soon. Never hit the ball until you have passed it unless you are compelled to do so for one of two reasons, either because somebody is coming up to interfere with the stroke by riding or hooking, or because it is crossing the goal and it is necessary to hit it before it reaches there, in which case distance is not the thing sought for but stopping the ball somehow. In these cases I swing with the hand held forward, making entirely a wrist stroke so as not to jab the ball down into the ground with a descending blow.

In making the back-stroke, particularly on the part of No. 4, care should be taken to hit the ball at some angle from the line of play in such a way that the stroke will not be blocked and spoiled by hitting oncoming horses. One well-known back, whom I knew, consistently drew the ball across behind his pony's quarters, hitting always toward his left, a policy which usually worked well.

The whole rush of ponies of both teams is following in the line the ball is coming, and if the stroke goes directly back there is a probability of hitting the feet or legs of one of the ponies or of the ball getting hit by the mallet of some alert opponent, whereas if the ball is drawn or cut by No. 4, when he backs it, so that it moves somewhat away from the line the crowd is following, there is every chance that it will not be blocked. Knowing this practice on the part of the player of whom I speak, I always threw my pony across to my left in order to intercept the ball, but rarely succeeded in blocking the back stroke, as I was across the new line the ball was traveling and the chance of blocking it was infinitely less than if I had been traveling along the line of the ball. The best players, however, look to see where they are hitting to and stroke to hit either to the right or to the left, according as they are hitting away from the goal they are defending, away from players of the opposing side, or toward players of their own side. Sometimes, perhaps all three considerations may enter into the thing, sometimes one and sometimes another being a controlling reason for the direction and distance of the stroke. When the ball is to be drawn across behind your own pony's quarters, it is well to ride fairly close to the ball, hitting a little later than you otherwise would, leaning back in the saddle and swinging well across behind the pony. The amount of the angle of swing to the line of the ball should be determined by the distance across it is desired to send the ball. If it is desired to send it well across, I should combine the cut or turned mallet head with the cross swing.

3. *The near-side stroke forward*— To make my near-side forward stroke, I stand up in the saddle. For this purpose I have my stirrups fairly short and turn so that my shoulders are parallel to the direction the horse is going. I then lean forward just enough to get my shoulder fairly well over the ball I am trying to hit and make what is really a back stroke forward. In other words, I use the same strength, muscle, and stroke, with my thumb down the center of the stick, as though I were hitting a back stroke on the off side, and in this way I get a lot of force in the near-side forward stroke. The swing is exactly the same as for the off-side back stroke, except that there is no occasion to put so much speed in the swing, as the momentum is now all in favor of the stroke. In order to get this position one has to make movements of the legs which, until the pony understands what is wanted, are likely to make her think she is wanted to turn; and, as a matter of fact, I have often seen ponies turn over the ball in response to the movement of the legs in making this stroke. This tendency may be balanced by a counter pressure of the rein, but a thoroughly trained pony, the moment she sees your hand swing across, will know that it means she is expected to stay straight and bring you up true on the ball, in spite of the fact that you have turned and changed the position of your legs in the saddle. I always move my mallet over to the near side as soon as I have decided to make the near-side stroke, so as to give my pony notice of what I expect of her. The tendency to hit late of the near side is even more pronounced than it is on the other side, owing to the length of time it takes to get placed and the increased difficulty in the stroke and the fact that one does not get the speed in the swing that is usual on the off side. Beginners should try to discount this by beginning their strokes a little sooner than it looks as though they ought to.

4. *The near-side stroke backward*— The back stroke on the near side is almost the most powerful stroke a player can make. It gets all the muscular force of a forward stroke on the off side. The only difficulty is that of gauging the distance from the ground. The swing, augmented by the turn of the body, gives an opportunity for immense force to the stroke. Here again caution is given in regard to hitting too soon. The same tendency that shows itself in hitting too late on the forward strokes leads a great many players to make the very serious error of hitting too soon on the back stroke. In all these strokes the mallet should make one complete circle. The stroke should always be carried through until the mallet is in the perpendicular.

To get practice in meeting coming balls, I recommend the exercise of having balls thrown toward oncoming pairs, in order than they may meet them. Here, more than in any other stroke, the difficulty lies in hitting soon enough. If the player can place himself so that he is traveling in the line in which the ball is coming, he is certain to hit it, provided he can get his mallet off soon enough, swings true, and the ball does not bounce. Players would begin this exercise with the pony at a stand-still, so as to see at what distance from the ball it is necessary to begin swinging so as to get the mallet down at the right time. They should also study to get a little adroitness in moving the pony into a position that will bring the swing along the line in which the ball is coming rather than across it. When the eye is trained and enough experience has been gained to meet the ball regularly with the pony standing still, the next development is meeting a thrown ball by riding toward it, gradually increasing the speed. When the pony is moving fast, the difficulty in meeting is not much greater than if the pony is standing still or if the ball is standing still, provided always that the ball does not bounce. As explained elsewhere, it is much more difficult to meet the ball successfully with a cross stroke than with a stroke that follows the line in which the ball is coming, as it takes a much nicer calculation.

When the ball is standing still or moving very slowly and it is desired to change the direction of play or to hit it in a direction other than that in which the pony has been going it is well to turn the pony and get started on the new line it is proposed to establish before hitting the ball. This should always be done if the ball is stationary, unless the player is being hurried by one of the other side and has to ride straight at the ball in order to maintain right of way. In other words, if by turning before reaching the ball one loses their right of way and possibly their chance to hit; one should hit the ball while turning, or, if that cannot be done without fouling, ride straight at it, hit it, and turn to follow it afterwards. When the ball is standing still, or nearly so, turning before reaching it has the following advantages: First, the stroke is truer because you are hitting in the direction you are going and do not have to send the ball at an angle to the natural swing of the mallet. Second, it is easier to hit the ball because the horse, when turning, is learning and therefore brings you nearer to the ground on one side or farther on the other, which makes necessary an adjustment of the length of the stick. Third, one of the most important things of polo is maintaining the right of way once on it. If the pony is headed in the right direction when the ball is hit, there is no necessity of further turning, which usually means some delay in getting adjusted to the new direction. Thus, if all of these preliminaries can be attended to before the rush is started when the ball is once hit, the pony can go along with accelerated speed and make the advance very much more formidable than it will be if there are preliminaries to be attended to after hitting and before the right of way can be entered upon and maintained at speed. In these connections, when there is plenty of time and it is desired to change the direction of the play directly back instead of turning directly over the ball, the player should ride past it about ten or fifteen feet, turn the pony, and come back at it, so that when the player finally hits the ball he is traveling along the line of the new right of way and is all ready to continue the rush.

5. *The half stroke*— The half stroke is made by dropping the mallet until it is perpendicular to the ground, swinging it slowly backward and then swinging it along the ground slowly forward, being careful to hit the ball after the mallet has passed the perpendicular and the head of the mallet is on the upward swing. In case the exigencies of the stroke are such as to necessitate hitting the ball back of the saddle, the same result can be accomplished by leaning away back, holding the arm back behind the saddle, and swinging from there without the usual forward movement of the hand and arm, taking the ball only with a swing of the wrist. A little practice will show what distance can be secured with half strokes, and, in case the ball is not driven far enough to allow time to make the second a full stroke, it is easy to make a second half stroke. In other words, if there is not time before reaching the ball again to make a complete swing, or if there is not enough room for such swing, owing to the close proximity of other players, the half stroke may be repeated.

The half stroke is useful; first, where a short distance is desired, and second, where there is not room for the full stroke. The short distance is usually desired, first, when hitting strokes that cut the lines of play and that do not parallel them, as shown in Fig. 1—in other words, when taking the ball around; second, in hitting where there is an opponent clear in front to whom you do not want to hit and who may be avoided by hitting short so that one cannot get near the ball without stopping or perhaps turning one's horse, in which case you have a good chance to rush past the player with your second stroke; third, hitting when it is desired to hit to some player of your side who can be reached by a short stroke but not by a long one; and fourth, in playing approach shots to goal. I am personally much opposed to taking long shots at goal. I believe in approaching and then sending the ball over from near to. I personally never try to hit a goal from a greater distance than sixty yards, even though directly in front and with a clear field. I always try an approach shot instead and then endeavor to drive the ball over, with my last stroke, close to. The reason for this is that hitting from over sixty yards requires such accuracy and precision of stroke that a player of no greater accuracy of stroke than I will probably knock the ball out; and I believe that team will win in the long run which plays always for approach to the goal, with the idea of hitting the ball through from fairly close to the goal line. The distance from which a goal may be safely tried varies with the angle. At a sharp angle one should not try the goal at a greater distance than thirty yards; at a very sharp angle it does not pay to try to hit the goal at all. I hit to have the ball stop out in front of the posts, depending upon a second stroke to carry it through.

There are certain niceties of play one sees in very expert players. One is dropping the mallet in the way of the ball so as to stop a long pass from one of your side from passing up to an opponent who is clear, thus preventing its return and placing it in position for some one of your side to take along. Another play is deliberately to dribble the ball toward your own goal so as to elude the rush of an oncoming opponent, and then to turn on it, passing it or backing it as the case may be. There are times when both of these devices are extremely effective.

To lift the ball one leans so as to swing the mallet head nearer the ground and hits a little bit sooner on the forward stroke and later on the back stroke. I have also found that a slight cut helps me to raise the ball; why, I don't know. I am not a believer however, in hitting into the air. Where one is aiming for the goal and there are players interposing, a small mathematical calculation will show that the chance of having a ball blocked at the height of the horse's body is many times greater than along the ground, where only the legs and feet of the ponies are in the way.

Greater distance may be obtained by raising the ball, thereby lessening friction, but when the ball falls it bounces so that it is more difficult for a rider in front to pick it up. A great distance is useful only when the ball is hit up by the backs, either on forward or back strokes. A back who raises the ball slightly gets the greatest distance; and the back who places it so as to be avoided by oncoming players is of greatest use to their side.

One often sees players who habitually miss their last stroke for goal after carrying the ball successfully for several strokes. This is usually due to their taking the eye off the ball to sight for the posts and not getting it back to the ball in time. Care should be taken to remedy this defect where it develops.

I consider it to be bad polo to knock the ball over the back line anywhere outside the posts.

I always carry the loop of the mallet over the wrist—never over the thumb. When placed over the wrist the mallet may be spun around a few times to twist the loop so it will not fall down over the hand when the hand is held down; but is should not be twisted enough to bind on the wrist.

When not hitting, the mallet should always be carried perpendicularly, and with the head up except when it is pretty certain that a half stroke will be needed shortly. A moment's thought will disclose the necessity of this, from the point of view of saving the muscles of the hand and arm, for, no matter how easy the play, it is a strain to hold the stick throughout the hour of play. The stick should be perpendicular because that is the easiest way to hold it. It takes almost no muscle to balance it, and it takes muscle to hold it in any other way except with the head directly down; but when held in this position the mallet is of no use when the time comes to hit a full stroke, as it has to be raised to the perpendicular before the stroke.

Especial care should be taken to learn how to hook an opponent's mallet successfully. Players should remember that a stroke spoiled is equal in value, although opposite in effect, to a stroke made. The clever use of the stick to spoil one's opponent's strokes is an asset easy to obtain, and it is a part of the necessary equipment of a first-class polo player.

I have found that to hook successfully it is wise to hold the mallet with the outer end of the head up in order that the opponent's mallet stroking the slope of the head may be brought into the stick and thus caught. Wherever possible the mallet should be hooked either at the beginning of the stroke or before the head has swing below the horizontal, as, if caught at the point where the mallet strokes the ball, the impact is apt to ruin both sticks.

There are so many chances in hooking that as a general rule of play I should personally recommend no player to hook the opponent's mallet in preference to riding their opposing player if in position to do so.

In playing, remember that ponies are apt to get discouraged by being hurt by a stroke of the stick, particularly at the beginning of their play. The player should so use their stick as to defend his head as well as his pony. A player should so hold it as to catch any stroke liable to land on the pony's head, and also to fend off strokes liable to get by and strike her in the nose, and, when necessary, the legs, although the legs are ordinarily protected by the boots—and strokes on the feet do not matter. It is the whip at the end of the stroke that ordinarily does the damage both to the player and pony, and it is always well to remember this and try to protect the face and eye by holding the stick conveniently. I never use the mallet for defense, however, when it may be needed for strokes.

While great strength is not necessary for polo, as some slight men of not great physical strength are among the best players and women increasingly occupy important spots on a polo team, at the same time it can be readily understood that strength of the hand is of utmost importance. Players who have not strong hands should take regular exercises calculated to strengthen the grip of the hand, wrist, and forearm. There are machines for this purpose, to be found in well-appointed gymnasiums, and personal devices can be purchased by which the grip of the hand is worked against a spring.

CHAPTER VI

TEAM PLAY

The cosmos of polo is difficult to understand because of the kaleidoscopic nature of the game and the fact that with each changing stroke the whole order of the game may be changed. This is inherent in the nature of the game, owing to the rapidity of the movement of the ball and of the players. It is none-the-less true that there is a very definite cosmos, and the fact that is difficult to grasp makes it more subtle, more intricate, and perhaps all the more important.

To determine the lines of greatest efficiency in playing, draw the polo field with lines radiating from the center of the offensive goal line and running straight till they have reached the sides, drawing no lines, however, that reach the side lines nearer the nearest corner of the field than is the line from the center of the goal line to the corner. If the field where straight-sided this would leave a right-angled triangle, which should be shaded or touched to a different color to indicate that it is what is known as dead territory, (Fig. 1)so called because it is out of the direct line of attack toward the goals. It is very bad polo for an attacking ream to send the ball into the dead territory except for special cause, as shown elsewhere.

The lines immediately in front of the defensive goal should go directly toward the sides, but the farther they get from the goal the more they should slant forward until at about sixty yards they should go directly up the field and toward the offensive goal. These lines to the sides should curve toward the offensive goal as they approach the side lines until they merge with the direct lines radiating out from the goal. The field will now be covered with a series of lines taking a general pear shape.

These lines indicate the correct line of travel for the ball. With a few exceptions, to be noted later, all strokes that cut these lines are bad polo; all strokes that parallel these lines are good polo.

There are three factors which control the position of the players. The first is the direction of the play, which in turn is controlled by the position and movement of the ball. The second is the spacing or position of the players on their own side. The third is the position of the opponents, particularly the corresponding one.

To make myself entirely clear, I will state that the corresponding opponent of No. 1 is No. 4, the corresponding opponent of No. 2 is No. 3; of No. 3, No. 2; and of No. 4, No. 1, and should be so understood wherever reference is made to a corresponding opponent. It does not always follow that the corresponding opponent will be the player who ought to be at that position. I am talking now always of the player who is IN that position; for instance, if in the exigencies of play the opposing No. 1 and No. 3 change places, No. 2's position will then be to play against the opposing No. 1.

Taking these three controlling factors up in order, the player should figure in his mind's eye the definite location of a "right of way" which extends along a line drawn through the center of the ball and, following the direction it is going, reaches from ten to forty feet in front of the ball, according to the speed of the play, and trails along behind it an indefinite distance. This right of way is four or five feet wide, or the amount of room taken up by the pony and a player with a clear swing of the mallet about one foot to the side of the ball.

The secret of team play is for a team to get quickly into the right of way the moment it is made possible by the movement of the ball and then come along with such speed as to maintain it, each player covering that section of the right of way which pertains to their position, and at the same time preventing the corresponding opponent from getting the ball.

The best way to teach players to respect the right of way is to let them understand that the person who has it will come down it at railroad speed, that is as disastrous to cross it as it is to cross a railroad track with an express train coming. The player who does not respect the right of way in good polo will get killed or cursed off the field before he has been at it many hours. All players who are outside of the line of play, except when they have moved out to cover an opponent so as to keep him out of it, are out of place and of no use to their team. This, however, does not apply to players who, under signal or pre-concerted arrangement, are placing themselves for a diagonal pass. Any player who gallops parallel to another of his own side is absolutely worthless to their team, as under no usual combination of circumstances can the ball be expected to pass sideways from the line which it is traveling; and anyone finding themselves riding in this way should immediately either pull up or call to the other team member to do so.

Players should never carry the ball around the field, except to defend goal or to avoid hitting it to one of the opponents who is clear and not covered by one of their own side. In the latter case the ball should be dribbled around with short strokes, preferably not more than fifteen or twenty feet to a stroke. Hitting long strokes around the fields has many disadvantages, but only one possible advantage. The possible advantage comes in the case of a very brilliant hitter who has a pony so very much faster than any pony on the field that he can, by hitting it far, get clear for the second stroke, being hard pressed at the time he first hits the ball. This condition is infrequent that it may be disregarded. The disadvantages are, first, that the play does not bring one any nearer to the goal which is sought; second, that the second stoke is at a difficult angle and must be taken either by turning the pony and hitting a cross the line of the ball or by hitting the ball at a sharp angle. The same is true of the third stroke, and, when the ball is afterwards brought around, the goal often has to be made at a difficult angle. Besides the difficulty of completing the play, it is one which is so easy to stop that an experienced player is seldom guilty of attempting it. A trained opponent will characterize it as "fruit", and sizing up the fact that one has an inexperienced player to deal with; will start across the field to intercept the next stroke before the player who made the stroke gets there. The opponent can usually start across first because the player who takes the ball around has to complete their stroke before they can turn their pony, whereas the opponent can start as soon as he sees where it is intended to send the ball, and, judging the relative speed of the ponies, he can so direct his course as to intercept the ball at any point in the circle which he feels he can reach. By getting there well ahead of the player who hit the ball across, one can break up the whole play and very likely get the ball and turn it to their own advantage. Other things being equal, if I see any of my opponents in a match develop the practice of taking the ball around, I know that they are certainly doomed to defeat.

In regard to spacing, this most important item of polo seems to be very difficult to impress upon beginners. A fundamental rule of team play is that no two players of the same side should be near or on the ball at the same time. The only exception to this rule is in the case of a player riding up to keep an opponent who he is covering from getting the ball, in which case he is covering his man and not riding for the ball. Even when covering an opposing player, if the ball is standing still and the players in front are standing over it and jabbing at it, he had much better let his corresponding player ride in and have a whack at it than to go in himself and join the mess. If a player lets the opponents bunch and then pulls up and takes his position, when the ball is hit out, the side which is spaced has three players that may get it, whereas the side which is not spaced has two. If two of these three players were covering their men as they ought to be doing, it means that the player who is free will get the ball and have a clear run of it. Players should understand they cannot help one of their own side who is on the ball except by doing one of three things—by putting themselves in the place to which the next stroke will send the ball; by coming right behind to take it in case it is missed, always being careful to stay far enough back to cover the corresponding opponent; or by riding an opponent and keeping him out of the play.

The distance that players should space from each other varies greatly with conditions. It depends upon the length of stroke of the player with whom you are playing, upon the speed of play, and upon the position occupied by the opponents. The exact point where the player should leave his opponent and ride back or forward to get his spacing is a thing which is hard to determine by rule and must depend upon the player's judgment, and the player's decision will differ according to the speed, skill, and mounts of himself and opponents, and to the style of play of the particular player from whom he is spacing, the distance of his strokes, etc. It also depends very largely upon the other players of the same side. For instance, if No. 2 has an extremely active and alert No 1, who is quite likely to turn and get the ball first in case the opposing back and he ride over it and he finds that No. 3 on the other side likes to ride close up, supporting his man from too close a distance, No. 2 may elect to ride in with the opposing No. 3 and break up his support of his team, confident that, if No 4 or

No. 3 of his own side get the ball back, his No. 1 will turn it to offensive account. There merit of this play also depends upon the part of the field in which it occurs. Where his goal is threatened, No, 2 should always ride in and block the opposing No. 3. If, however, the goal is not threatened and the play is well up in the field, and he thinks No. 3 is riding up too close, No. 2 may lurk the proper distance back to receive the ball.

One team that I have seen play, which has excellent team work, always has No. 2 lurk away back on the defense, counting on No. 3 and No. 4 getting the ball back to him. This, however, is counting on erroneous play on the part of the opposing No. 3, who, if he knows his business, will pull up and instead of following close to his No. 2, will support him from a space of, say, five yards or so in front of his lurking opponent, who offensive value will thus be nullified. No. 3, so playing, would be pretty sure to get the ball in case the opposing No. 4 sends it well back, and he still would be in position to come through on it in the case the two pairs in front ride over it.

Supporting one's own players by following too close is also dangerous. Many runs are spoiled by the ball bouncing in the air. If the ball bounces and hits the stick it is pretty sure to go sideways. If a player is following the man in front too closely that the ball hits the stick and goes a little to one side or hits the pony's feet and stops or bounces back (as it is very apt to do when two players are riding each other over it), the checked movement of the ball will throw a closely pursuing player entirely out. If the corresponding opponent, riding further back, is not covered, he will come along and get the ball. Thus, No. 2, for example, trailing along, expecting his No. 3 or his No. 4 to send the ball back or ride over it and leave it for him to take, should ride with his eye alternately watching the players in front and the opposing No. 3 who should be beside or behind him. He should pull up and space himself as not to be thrown entirely out by a sideways movement or check of the ball. At the same time, if the ball is sent well back, he will cover the opposing No. 3 and not leave him riding clear so that he can get the ball. In other words, the spacing in a case like that is controlled almost entirely by the position of the corresponding player on the other side, unless he is so ridiculously far back as to be out of place.

In play of average speed, 30 to 35 yards is fair spacing. Players should always begin to get nervous the minute they begin to get within 15 yards of any of their side. The secret of effective team work in any game is so to direct your play that the fault will be less with you than with any other player; in other words, be sure to do your part.

Many players, particularly those who have recently begun the game, get what is known as "ball crazy." They have one idea fixed in their heads, and that is the ball; they must be on it all the time. They cannot realize that a person can be of any use to his team unless he is hitting the ball. One of the commonest manifestations of this mania is the practice of backing the ball when the opponents have hit it so that it is about to roll over the back line. Good players always let it roll over. It means that the whole team will get their ponies turned and get ready for the offensive rush before the ball is hit rather than afterwards. The knock in is almost certain to be a better stroke than a back stroke when the ball is moving with the uncertainty of bouncing, etc. All the arguments are in favor of letting the ball go out. Also the opponent's safety should be allowed to go over except in the exceptional circumstance of a good shot at goal as it rolls or in the event of the last few minutes of a game where a goal is needed to win and the ball can be placed where a probable goal will result.

It is axiomatic that a stroke spoiled is equal to a stroke made. The player who cannot hit the ball well may very easily be of equal use to their side by preventing the opponents from hitting it. It should be the ambition of each player, however, to do a little bit more than his share, to be a little bit better than the corresponding player on the other side. A player should not be satisfied to be an entirely negative quantity neutralizing the work of some person of the other side; he should also be a positive force. In calculating the merit of a player, however, one must always remember that no amount of brilliant work will compensate for failure to cover properly the corresponding opponent. Thus the person playing No. 2 should know instinctively every minute of the time just where the opposing No. 3 is. By opposing No. 3 I mean, as I have said before, the person playing No. 3's position. He should have an uncomfortable feeling that it is his fault every time the opposing No. 3 hits the ball. If he is supporting his own man, the distance he follows him up must be controlled by the position the opposing No. 3 is playing.

There are two ways of riding off. One is to watch the corresponding opponent and play your pony so as to cover his every movement. The other is to play for the ball, and having first placed yourself where you can reach it before your opponent, get there first when the time comes, watching his every movement and making sure that you are constantly holding your pony in such a position as to cover the point from which the corresponding opponent can be harmful to your side. When the time for the rush comes, however, you should play directly for the ball, thus putting your opponent on the defensive and making him ride you instead of your riding him, but guiding yourself by covering the point at which he can be harmful to your side. Both methods must be used from time to time, but of the two the latter is very much the more scientific and effective. It really compels your opponent to ride you instead of your riding him. It puts the burden of effort on him. It is the old story that strong offense is the strongest defense. I use both methods. If I have nothing better to do and my opposing No. 3 is not looking, I am very apt to place my pony across his or place myself in such a position against his pony that my knee is in front of his knee. This is the best way to ride off. You want so to arrange that the pressure of all four legs of your pony is against the forelegs of the opponent's pony. This makes a pressure of four against two and means that you can push him off provided your pony is any good at pushing. The player so covered will undoubtedly try to extricate himself. Sometimes it is well to let him, having delayed him for some time, in order to give him another similar scrap when he again tries to pass. Sometimes it is better to stay by him, all depending upon circumstances. If he is so far out of position as to limit his usefulness, it is not worthwhile to stay with him at the expense of leaving a gap in your own position. If, however, he is in his position, then your proper play is a series of maneuvers and jockeying, just as important and delicate as the jockeying of race horses at the start of a race or the maneuvering for position at the start of a yacht race.

Each player should try to be a little in front of the corresponding opponent, whichever way the ball is going. If he does this successfully, it involves quick work when the ball is backed and the direction of play turns from toward one goal to the other, for the player who was ahead must do some sharp riding to pass his man as he turns, and, after turning, to get once more to his coign of vantage.

When playing, however, the rules as to position have to give way to immediate need. The player who is nearest the ball must get to it, even though out of position, rather than let one of the other side get it, in which case it is usually necessary for the person who should have been at that position to pass and take up the place left by the player who rides to the ball. This, however, is qualified by the necessity of observing whether the one who is in place is in position to get the ball. For instance, suppose two players of one side both can reach the ball before one of the opponents, it is clearly the duty of one or the other to take the ball, and the one who does not take it should pull up or ride on and take his position, regardless of the fact that he may be able to get the ball first, unless the advantage to be gained is so manifest as to justify changing positions and the change is called and accepted.

A player, however, should always stay by any opponent whom he has covered, if such opponent is in position to be in immediate danger to the play.

On the throw in No. 1, No. 2, and No. 3 should be on their side of the line with their ponies facing diagonally toward the line, generally toward the referee; No. 4 should take up a place ready for an offensive or defensive rush half way between No. 2 and No. 3, and from ten to fifteen yards away from the line, ready to gallop directly back in case any of the front players of the opposing side get the ball, and he should rush for it himself in case the ball rolls past No,. 3. No. 3 in this case should follow defensively in case his No. 4 gets it, holding himself ready to ride back in case the rush should be unsuccessful and leave the ball exposed to any of the opponents. When the ball is thrown in, the player should drive his pony fiercely at it as though the whole game depended on it, trying to push his pony across the line. I have often swung at the ball, timing my stroke to the movement of the ball, hoping to hit it as it passed under, without seeing it, and often have found the result was a good sharp stroke down the field. Don't slash recklessly with your mallet, as it is too likely to hit one of your opponents. Players should always be considerate of the chance of a mallet head reaching an opponent and try to avoid such contingencies.

Each player failing to get the ball should see that his vis-à-vis does not get it. Once the ball has passed, however, he can ride to his position, which should always be in a line up and down the field. The moment the ball has passed No. 1 he should ride instantly to the opposing back, riding fast so as to get there in case No. 2 or No. 3 should send the ball up to him.

When the ball is hit, all players should figure in their mind's eye the line of the right of way and either get into it or get parallel to and ahead of one of the opposing player, so as to be in position to neutralize his efforts.

The essence of first-rate play is hitting the ball straight down the field. In first-rate polo the ball will be traveling perpendicularly up and down the field at a maximum and across the field at a minimum. It is well for players to train themselves always to play the best polo, which means taking the ball up and down the field and backing it when it is desired to turn it rather than taking it around.

No. 3 or No. 4 may do the knocking in according to which is the stouter hitter. The ball should always be knocked away from the goal and toward the side-boards. The rush for the attack should start from the side-boards, never from the center, where any miss or block would leave the goal in danger. The balance of chance is all against the team whose goal is threatened. Hit to the sides and then start the rush for the opposing goal from the side-lines or from a point near the sides where the team is in position to get a good start down the field. When No. 4 knocks in, No. 3 should place himself about 10 yards in the field and between the ball and the goal posts, and let No. 4 ride through on his first stroke, No. 3 staying back to defend in case any return of the ball threatens the goal. He should follow No. 4 up in case the latter hits the second stroke, in order not to be too far out of the play. Keene, however, believes No. 3 should play well out.

No. 2 should place himself next to the boards, well back toward the goal line, and should pick up No. 4's hit as it strikes the side boards and endeavor to carry it down the field.

No. 1 should place himself alongside of the opposing No. 4 and stick to him like a leech.

Crane suggests a line-up for a knock in in which No. 3 takes up a position about half way between the ball and No. 2. This puts the team in regular position and sends the whole team down the field on the ball. This formation has much to commend it.

The knock in may be varied by a series of plays called for by signal. One of these is to have the No. 2 take their position near the side boards and close to the back line; instead of No. 4 knocking in, No. 2 gallops very rapidly across and comes at the ball, going at full speed, and hits it across goal to No. 3, who has left his position in front of the posts and has gone out to pick it up. No. 4 follows No. 2 to carry the ball along in case No. 2 hits poorly or misses. In this case No. 3, No. 2, and No. 4 are in line on the ball, going at full speed, a combination particularly well adapted to a successful and aggressive attack. This may be varied, if the other side get rushing across the field to meet this play as soon as they see No. 2 starting to gallop, by having No. 4 wait behind the posts and No. 2 make a feint to hit the ball and pass over it while No. 4 waits until he has passed and then knocks it out toward the side boards as in the regular knock in, and follows it up to take it along down the boards,. When the opponents are well under way across the field into the cross-goal territory, No. 3 and No. 2 turn to get back, if possible before the opponents, and thus support their No. 4. No. 1 in this play never starts across at all and waits to pick the ball up in case No. 4 sends it down the field successfully.

Other variations of this play may be tried successfully. One of them is for No. 4 to hit the ball along the back line and No. 2 to pass it out diagonally and cross the field where No. 3 can be waiting for it. Under no circumstances should a team make any play that does not have the resultant object of starting a rush to goal from fairly close to the side-line.

Where the opposing side is knocking in, No. 1 should ride in and try to meet the ball from about 30 yards out.

No. 2 should be out toward goal to take the ball if it is passed to him and also to defend in case an attempt is made to knock in across the goal.

No. 2's position will vary with the position of the ball on the back line; if it is near the boards he will take a position slightly to the side of the goal from a line through the ball and perpendicular to the back line.

No. 3 should be on the boards defending and No. 4 toward the boards but nearer the center of the field and little farther back than No. 3.

When the ball is knocked into the offensive corners, No. 2 is clearly the player who should ride in. No. 1 or No. 3 should never go in after it unless they happens to be next to the opponent who has the best chance to get the ball and No. 2 is not in position to do it themselves. In this case, No. 1 or No. 3 should call to No. 2 that he is riding in, so that No. 2 will not do so. In the defensive corners, No. 2 must expect to go in, although it is often No. 3's duty to ride in, in which case No. 2 takes their place on the diagonal line, as showed in Fig. 22. No two players of the same side should ever ride in, either to get the ball or to impede an opponent. The rest of the team should line up on the diagonal line (Figs. 1 and 22) which represents the line between live and dead territory, and take position, watching for the ball to come out.

No. 1's position in the offensive corners is nearest goal. In the defensive corners this position is usually determined by the opposing back, but in general it can be said to be near the side lines on the line between dead and live territory.

The team should understand that the corners of the field are dead territory, and —unless the play is sent into the corners for the purpose of wasting time, as might be the case toward the end of a game which was well in hand and in which the ponies were beginning to tire, or in case a player of your side has gone to get a new stick or mount—that hitting to the corners, in so far as its offensive value to the team is concerned, is worse than not hitting the ball at all. But many players, particularly beginners, seem to think that they must hit the ball, even though the stroke they make is from the goal they are trying to hit, and that their part of the play is done if they hear the crack of their stick against the ball. There are many times in polo when not hitting at all is much better strategy than hitting. This is the case with a stroke that throws the player out of the effective line of play (Fig. 1) that puts the player at a point where the goal is at a difficult angle and where turning the pony to get a shot at goal makes a difficult stroke, or when to hit the ball would hit to an opponent who is clear, or when one of his own side is in a better position to take it.

One other important item of play is that which is commonly known as "hitting short." Let us say that No. 3 is away with the ball and that No. 1 and his opposing No. 4, and No. 2 and his opposing No. 3, are in front of him. No.2 is trying to cover the corresponding opponent but is not in position to do so. No. 3 is on the ball and his corresponding opponent, we will say, is lurking behind waiting for something to happen. If No. 3 hits a long stroke, the opposing No. 3 or No. 4 will be pretty sure to send it back, but by hitting it a short stroke, just up to the tail of the nearest opposing pony, then going up on it fast, he puts the opposing player in the uncomfortable position of deciding either to pull up, in which case he will make a rush past him, or to gallop on to get the next stroke, in which case another short stroke will answer the purpose. The only way such a play can be properly stopped is for the No. 2 of the opposing side to wake up to their responsibilities and ride up and block the play from behind; in other words, to ride his man, a thing he ought to have been doing all the time. If this play is a good one when the players in front are partially covered, it is still better where a player finds himself by chance with the opposing back or the opposing No. 3 uncovered. Of course, the defense then is for the uncovered player to pull up and immediately ride the person who has made the short stroke, leaving it to the players behind to come up and get the ball, in which case he trusts to his own teammates to be in place and do their part, which is correct polo strategy.

One of the most important items of team play is the signaling from player to player, which it is very hard to get even experienced players to do, yet in my judgment it is one of the most necessary components of successful polo.

I use the following general calls, and while I am constantly calling to the players of my side, I am at the same time listening for their words.

The most important signal of all is "Leave it," which I usually repeat very loud until the player has obeyed, saying "Leave it," "Leave it," "Leave it." This is a direct order to the player of your side not to hit it, and should never be given because the one who calls for the other players to leave it thinks he is a better player, but only because he has a better angle on the ball and is in a better position to hit it, or because there is an opponent clear in front who will get the ball if it is not left but is hit by the forward player.

"Go on" should never be used when "Leave it" is meant, because "Go on" may mean to go on with the ball or without it. "Go on" should be used by every player who is on the ball and is coming through and who wants the other players of their side to keep on in the direction they are going. It should be used from behind the player who is hitting the ball or by the one who fails to prevent an opponent hitting the ball. For instance, if in a defensive rush No. 1 fails to ride No. 4, he should call his side to "Go on," particularly if he sees any signs that his No. 2 is beginning to pull up, intending to turn, which will get him out of the play.

It is well to have a signal to indicate when there is plenty of time. Any word well understood by both teams will serve, such as "Plenty" or "Slowly." If the phrase "Take your time" is used sometimes players mistake it for a call for time and stop playing. It makes a lot of difference to players to know whether they are hurried or not; whether, for example, they will have time to turn on the ball or pull up their pony, or wait until the ball has stopped rolling or bring their stick up for a full swing, or wait until their own side has got in position before hitting.

"Ride your man" is an encouragement to a player which ought not to be needed. Every player ought to ride anyway without orders, but it is very often needed, especially among beginners and among players who think more of the ball than they do of the team.

When the ball turns, "Turn" or some signal understood by the team should be called, for the benefit of players in front who cannot see or who have not seen. The player closest to the ball when it turns should immediately call to their own side to turn.

Allan Forbes suggests that another word be used as signal to tell your players to turn. This is better, as it does not inform the other side; "Look out" or "Hold them" might serve.

"I am next" is a phrase which is sometimes useful. A player who is on the ball should know if one of their own side is clear and next. It may make a difference in the style of their play. For example, No. 2 is going down the side of the field and into one of the corners, and he does not know whether, if he misses it, No 3 of his side will get it or it will go to one of the opposing side. He cannot take his eye off the ball and yet his stroke will depend somewhat on whether he is supported or not. If he knows that his No. 3 is there to get the ball if he misses it, he will try a much more difficult turn stroke to get it in line toward the goal than he would undertake in case he were not sure but that the ball would go to the other side if he missed. Or he may make a turning stroke, placing the ball where he cannot reach it again, and then ride on to pick up the ball when it is sent along to him by his supporting player or to clear the way by riding out the opposing back or No. 3.

The signal "Back it" it also used under certain circumstances.

In the Dedham team we had a practice of using a signal when we wanted the ball backed or were planning to back the ball which did not give the play away; "Easy" or "Steady" or any agreed-upon word would serve.

Do not say the same thing in different ways; say it in the same way always. Do you say "Go on" when you mean "leave it." If you want them to go on, say "Go on." If you want them to leave it, say "Leave it." Do not give the gratuitous information "I've got it" or "I have it," which means nothing. I have noticed that players after boasting that extent are more than likely to lose it. One of the principal uses of this business of calling to your side is to help a player who is straining their every effort to ride off an opponent. He is timing his every move to match that of the horse of the player he is riding off, who, if he plays a scientific game, is very likely to pull up suddenly and cross behind the line of play and get the ball, timing his play by watching when his opponent is looking around to see what is happening behind. To anticipate this and not be put at a disadvantage, a player has to watch every single move made by his corresponding opponent. If, at the same time, he has to turn around and keep looking backward, to find out whether the ball is still coming, he is placed at a real disadvantage. If, however, he can depend upon his own players behind him to call "Go on" with each stroke, if the movement of the play continues, and "Turn" or its equivalent the second the direction of the play changes, he can do very much better work in riding off. This matter of keeping your teammates informed is one of the most important and least observed items of team play.

In a recent tournament, I saw No. 4 come through with the ball, never opening his mouth to let his team know that he had got it, and no less than five players pulled up and turned, assuming that, because No. 3 had missed, the rush had ended. Three of these players were of the attacking side, and No. 4's rush was completely nullified by the fact that he had to go through alone—all of his own players having given up—this being entirely due to the failure on his part to let them know beforehand what he himself knew and could perfectly well have told, namely, that he was next on the ball.

Of course, it is incumbent upon players to inform themselves even when they know they can depend on their own men; they ought to look around sometimes, even going so far as to turn their ponies in default of instructions from the players behind. But the necessity for looking around, as I have pointed out, results disastrously to the best riding off, and the players, instead of keeping on confidently at speed, are holding and expecting any minute that the time to turn will have passed without their having been looking at that particular moment.

In case, for any reason, you want one of your own side to take the ball, say "Take it." This is a direct sharp order to a player who should then leave his man, even against better judgment, and take the ball.

I remember that in one very difficult match I was playing against a New York team my No. 1 had the back covered and 20 feet off to one side. I was going along smoothly with nothing to prevent my taking the ball straight to goal, which, as the score was tied—13 all—and we were playing an extra chukker, would have won the game. At this juncture my mallet head broke. I heard the crack as I hit the ball, and looking down, saw the jagged crack running through the head and knew it would not last another stroke. I called to my No. 1 to "Take it," and galloped hard to get in position to cover his man as he left him. A poor player at No. 1 would have been undertaking to leave his man anyway so as to get a whack at the ball—an inexcusable play. A good player, not thoroughly disciplined, would have looked around to see what the matter was and asked an explanation before leaving his position, this player happened to be properly trained and instantly rode in an took the ball, without asking for an explanation, the result preventing what otherwise would have been disastrous.

In a scrimmage, when one or more ponies are standing, players on the outside should make a point of telling their player nearest the ball where it is, as "To your right," "Left," "Ahead of you," "Under you," etc. Often a player a little way off can see when the other cannot. It is well, whenever the ball has struck a pony's legs or made an unexpected movement, to assume that your teammate has not seen it, and to tell them, as sometimes an opportunity is lost by reason of a ball perfectly within reach not being seen. In such circumstances also the voice of the player gives the direction and lets the man know his whereabouts. In fact, it often pays to use some word or call when you are in position to receive a pass to help the player who is making the stroke, as he may not have time to look around to see where you are.

In order to assure certainty as to cooperation, a player, in passing out of their position to take that of another, should speak. For instance, No. 1 when riding past No. 2 should say "I am 2." Having said so, he should hold that position and assume its responsibilities and be ready to pass with No. 3 and not go back to his position without passing the word again to No. 2 and saying "I am 1." No. 2 should then accept the responsibility by replying. When No. 1 says "I am 2," No. 2 should hold No. 1's position until a favorable opportunity comes to pass, at which time he should respond to No. 1's calling "I am 1" by replying "I am 2." In other words, it should be understood and expected between players, after a change of position has been made, that each should assume the responsibility of the position until an opportunity comes to change back, when the fact of changing back and the reversal of responsibility has passed by word of mouth between the two. Similarly with No. 3 and No. 4 or with No. 2 and No. 3, in fact, similarly with the whole team. It is unusual for this practice to prevail in great changes of players. For instance, it is too upsetting to the team to have No. 1 as far out of place as at back, which probably means that every player is out of their place. No. 1 probably cannot do back's business for them safely. Unless goal is threatened or he is the next man to the ball, or keeping the threatening player of the other side off the ball, he should go right back to place, passing the word as he goes back. The best chance to change back to position comes when the ball goes out or over the boards, or when it is backed or taken around the field.

Every stroke should be made with a definite object. The player should get it into their head that there are two points of equal importance to the stroke. One is the point of beginning and the other is the point of ending, and he should not hit the first without having a very definite idea as to the second. My experience has led me to believe only one in about five strokes can be made at full speed the full distance of the stroke. This conclusion, however, is contested by men whose rating and experience qualify them to speak as masters of the game. They assure me that in the fastest polo full strokes are the rule and hitting short is usually impracticable. The player should always know before hitting where he is hitting to, where the players of his own side are and how to hit so that one of them can advantageously get to it, and, of course, so that the opposing side cannot reach it so easily.

In placing the ball so that it can be best reached by members of your team, there are some nice problems in angle hitting which players will do well to study most carefully. Here also are opportunities for exceptions to the rules laid down in connection with Figure 1, as it may very well be that hitting straight to goal will place the ball in such a way that the opposing back is sure to get it, whereas hitting fairly well to the right or left may put it easily within reach of your own covering player. A study of the diagram of Figure 25 will show how it is perfectly possible so to place the ball at an angle to the straight line to the goal as to give your own man in front of you a chance to reach the ball first, even though his opposing player is ahead of him. We'll say No. 2

has the ball. The opposing back is four to eight feet ahead of No. 1 and it is obvious No. 1 cannot catch up to cover him. If the ball is hit straight and far, there is no power that can prevent the opposing back from getting to the ball first and returning it. The opposing No. 3 is well mounted, and No. 2 knows that his chance of following the ball up and getting it again if he hits short is small. By hitting the ball at an angle to its course and to the side of the opposing back upon which his No. 1 has taken his position, be it right or left, if No. 1 is riding a little wide of his back, it can be easily brought about, as shown in the figure, that when both players in front are turned to reach the ball, No. 1 is nearer to it and can take the ball along, having the opposing back at a disadvantage.

If No. 2 sees that No. 1 is between him and the opposing No. 4, it is proper to hit short to let No. 1 get up and ride his player out; or in case the opposing back is incautious and plays too close, No. 1 can pass him and take the pass from his No. 2, who will send a long stroke up to him. But under such circumstances it never pays to try to make a long stroke for goal. Other details of this play will be given in the chapters on the various positions.

In order properly to comprehend the duties of each position, each player should learn the duties of all positions and play in each for a while. He should consider that each man's part in the team is just as important and just as distinct as are the various parts of a clock. The mechanism is just as nice and just as well adjusted. The limits of plays where one man's work can be effective are not hard and fast, as they vary with various conditions, yet with each condition his play is absolutely clearly marked.

In the first part of this chapter, I have indicated regular play. There are lines of attack other than regular straight up-and-down play which it sometimes pays to use.

One is a sudden shifting of the line of attack, when by either chance or design the ball is taken and turned towards the side lines. To carry it around is the obvious and usual way. To back it toward the center and somewhat toward the goal you are trying to defend, under a preconceived understanding with your men, establishing a new line of attack, is a very effective offensive movement. It takes the other side completely by surprise, unless they are looking for it, and is sure to succeed, given average execution unless each player of the opposing side instead of playing only for the ball is religiously covering his man, which is the only defense against this play. If a player sees his corresponding opponent siding off to another part of the field from that to which the ball would naturally go, he should take up a coign of vantage from which he can get to him, if necessary, before the ball does.

I have sometimes thought of working up an entirely new style of play with the lines of attack, by which the ball would be passed from one line to another by means of back strokes, or cross strokes, one of these parallel lines to be formed by No. 1 and No. 3 and the other by No. 2 and No. 4, each to be ready to rush, if occasion arose, or to pass the ball across. This passing across, however, presents difficulties. In the main, the simplest way of working this bit of strategy would be for some one player, where the ball is in the opponent's half of the field, deliberately to hit toward the boards. If the opposing players rush to block him when he reaches the ball, instead of taking it round at a difficult angle, at which he is pretty sure to give it to one of the other side before he gets it round, he should make a short stroke back somewhat toward the center of the field where his other players, knowing beforehand what is going to happen, are waiting for it. By hitting the ball once and establishing a new right of way toward the goal and holding it with a rush, they would have a very difficult style of play to meet and cope with, particularly if it has caught the opponents in such a position that they would have to get in such a position that they would have to get into the line of play at a sharp angle, a thing which it is difficult for anyone to do without fouling or losing a good deal of distance in turning, before getting where he can hit or interfere with an opponent. As I have said before, the only successful defense would be for each player to cover his opponent and not get led away in the wild delirium of a chase after the ball.

It is very bad polo to knock over the side line or over the back line except for a purpose.

Never make the practice of playing for your opponent's misses. That merely means that you may be temporarily successful against unskillful players, but it does not teach you good polo. Play as though your opponent were a good player. After the player has learned good polo, taking the easier and lazier course of playing to an opponent's blunders is done with the eyes open and knowing that it is incorrect polo—there is then not so much harm in it. But if a man learns to play for misses instead of riding his man, he will get into bad habits, which will be very disastrous to him in case of running up against the real thing.

In good polo, playing against good players, do not pull up and wait for the stroke of the one you are supposed to cover, but crowd them even though you are hopelessly behind. No one hits so well when hard pressed as they do when they have plenty of time, and the fact that you are crowding in will prevent his turning on it or taking time for their team to organize.

To all players: Ride! Ride! Ride! And again, Ride your man!

CHAPTER VII

DUTIES OF No. 1

No. 1 is the most difficult position on the field to play well, and a team that can afford to put a really first-class player at No. 1 is the most formidable team to meet. It is a position of tremendous possibilities. It follows that it requires superlative horsemanship, great devotion to the job of putting the opposing back out of play, and an utter unselfishness in the matter of leaving the ball for others behind to bring along. An excellent horseman, well mounted, not necessarily very experienced in the matter of hitting the ball, can be of the greatest use to the team by neutralizing the superior hitting qualities of the opposing back. By a curious contradiction No. 1 is usually the place selected for the putting the poorest player. This is because that is the place where they can do the least harm. The player is less needed on the defense, and can be extremely useful to the team if they ride well and hard and use their position to interfere with the opposing backs, not necessarily hitting the ball themselves.

No. 2's principal duty is to keep the opposing back out of the play. To accomplish this there are two methods of riding, which are explained in Chapter VI, "Team Play," page 71 hereof, and which I shall not repeat, except to indicate that one of them is by getting into and holding a strategic position and then riding for the ball. This I consider the most effective method of play and therefore most dangerous to the good work of the opponents, but one which is usually more applicable to the play of No. 2 and No. 3. The other is to ride the corresponding opponent direct. No. 1 can cover his position and save his ponies more than any other player. Allan Forbes played one pony ten years exclusively in that position, and often used only two ponies for his important matches. These important matches included matches for the championship of the United States and a great may other games against first class players. No. 1 should dispossess his soul of the idea that he has to be hustling all the time. He can pull up and wait when the ball is going around or turning, and should always take care to maneuver so as to be in position on the right or mallet side of the opposing back, so as to force him to take a high-side stroke if he wants to get the ball without getting crooked, and then wait, keeping an eye all the time on the movements of the opposing back and at the same time watching the ball.

The strategic place for No 1 to lie in is a comfortable berth a few yards off the off fore shoulder of the pony of the opposing back, always being a little ahead of him in the direction the ball is going. If he sees the back galloping forward, he can be sure that he should immediately gallop with him in order to block him all he can. In case of doubt, stick by your man.

On the throw in, No. 1 should place himself pretty well back from the referee and endeavor to get there before the No. 1 of the opposing side lines up. He should not move forward until about the time the ball is to be thrown, which he can guess pretty closely by counting slowly after the thirty second whistle is blown. About five seconds before the ball is thrown, he should get in place, with his pony a little nearer the referee than the other pony, if possible. As the ball is thrown, he should drive his pony heavily across the line, leaning pretty strongly against his opponent if he is in position to interfere, and endeavor to get the ball as it passes under. If he misses it and the other No. 1 gets it, he stays by him and rides him just as though he were the back until he has spoiled the rush. After the rush is spoiled he turns to see whether he can get to the ball quicker than any other player on his side. If he cannot, his job is to ride immediately to his position. If, on the other hand, on the thrown in, the ball passes by, No. 1 should immediately extricate himself from the opposing No. 1 and start to gallop fast toward the goal he is trying to make until he gets to an advantageous position near the opposing back, where he should stop and wait unless the movement of the ball or of the opposing back indicates that movement is necessary. If no. 2 comes along with the ball and drives it up past, while No. 1 has the opposing back well covered, No. 1 should assume that No. 2 is in position to take it again and should stay by his back unless he hears a call from his own man to take it, or unless, looking around, he sees that No. 2 has been passed by one of the opponents who will get the ball, in which case he is free to ride for the ball, but in such case No. 2 should have directed him to "Take it." If No. 1 has got his opposing back covered and crowded out of the line of play, unless thoroughly drilled and conversant with his duty, he will have an almost irresistible impulse to leave the man he has so nicely covered and turn and go to the ball as it comes up past him. To do this when No. 2 has hit it last and is clear behind, is nothing short of criminal, the penalty for which should be at least six years at hard labor in the penitentiary. No. 1, if he has his opposing No. 4 covered, is doing everything that could be expected of him. If No. 2 hit it last, the presumption is that he is in position to hit it again, as, given equal ponies and equal horsemanship, No. 3 of the other side cannot catch up to interfere. If, however, he does, there is always the fair chance that his No. 3 will be following and able to take the ball along. If No. 1 turns and leaves his player to get the ball, his opponent will do one of two things: He can either run and crook No. 1's stick and then take the ball himself, or, as No. 1 turns to get into the line of the play, he can gallop hard and get past No. 1 and back the ball on the next stroke. Moreover, it is somewhat difficult to extricate your pony from riding off another, as a pony, when leaning well over and well braced against another pony, usually objects a little to changing and resists for a moment the effort of his rider to make him leave an opposing pony, a tendency which does credit to his intelligence as a strategist and one from which an open-minded No. 1, not swelling with the conceit that he is superior to brute creation, might draw some valuable points on how to play his position. In fact, it is usually necessary to spur a pony away in order to make him leave another that he is leaning against, which takes a little time. Having gone away from the player he is riding, No. 1 then has to turn to get to the ball and turn against or get along the line of play. All of these processes usually result in No. 1's freeing the back, as before explained, and reaching the ball just in time to make a poor stroke and to interfere with his own No. 2 who is riding free along the line of play and could have hit it without any of the maneuvers which have spoiled No. 1's direction and without the added disadvantage of leaving the opposing back clear ahead and in position to spoil the whole play.

On the defense, No. 1 should stay by back, gauging his distance and position by that of his opponent, and always ride through with him in case he rushes forward, provided that he can interfere with his play and that his opponent is on the ball as he goes through. If the opposing back is riding up on some mistaken theory that he had better get in and help somebody, No. 1 should stay back and hold his place, spacing himself on No. 2. Unless he has a chance to prevent his opposing No. 4 making a stroke, he should never ride in with him past the opposing No. 3.

Where the opposing No. 3 and No. 4 change places, No. 1 and No. 2 should change with their men if by doing so they can prevent one of them making a stroke, otherwise, they had better hold their places and let No. 1 take the opposing No. 3 and No. 2

take the opposing No. 4. In other words, there is no sense in changing position unless there is something to be gained by doing so, and the only thing to be gained is to spoil the stroke or rush of the opposing side. There are times when the whole two teams could change ends, such as where the ball is brought by one side down the side of the field and, when hit across toward goal, picked up by the back of the other side and carried ahead around the field, and down the other side. In that case, if each player should ride his man, both teams would find themselves changed end for end, but as a matter of fact this practically never occurs, as No. 4, the moment he sees the opposing No. 4 hitting around, will always cut across to defend goal instead of following the circle. In this case No. 1 has to watch his chance and cut back. Probably he will find that the opposing No. 4, as soon as the rush is checked, has turned to get back too, for all good No. 4's have an anxious feeling about the goal they are defending and won't stay up in the game long.

Fig. 20 represents a case where the three opposing players have ridden over the ball. No. 1 finds himself, as he should be, a little ahead of the opposing back, who, seeing that he cannot get to the ball first, instead of riding in pulls up and waits for No. 1's stroke. Under no circumstances should No. 1 hit the ball to the waiting back. He has two or three courses open, all depending on circumstances. The first and the most usual one is to stop and stand over the ball with his pony facing across the field, always being sure that there is no possibility that No. 4 will rush in and make him commit a foul by so doing. No. 2 and No. 3 of his side will turn and get to him just as quickly as possible. The first one of these to get around should be No. 2, who, seeing him standing this way, should pass him at a little distance and receive the ball by a light tap across the field, the ball slanting, however, toward the goal to be made, but not slanting enough so that the opposing back will have any chance for it. No. 1 could then follow No. 2, and, in case the opposing back has by that time got so that he could reach the ball as it comes from the next stroke of No. 2, No. 1 could call upon No. 2 to leave it and take the back, and No. 1 come along on the ball playing No. 2.

Another play that No. 1 may make under the circumstances indicated above is to turn on the ball and take it himself. In this case, if No. 4 stays quite a distance back, No. 1 should ride past the ball, all the time watching to make sure No. 4 doesn't ride up and steal the ball, and then turn and advance back on it, getting the pony well under way before he reaches the ball. He is now in position to vary his play according to circumstances. He can hit it just short of the back and follow it up by another stroke, or, if his No. 2 gets around in time, he can hit it a short stroke and then ride over it, going up to his position and letting No. 2 come up and take the ball along. What I have said elsewhere about following up other players too close applies with equal force to No. 1. When on the defensive, he should never follow up the players in front so close as to let the opposing No. 4 trail and thus stand any chance of the ball being deflected so that he will ride over it and leave it to the opposing back; in fact, he should always stay back and cover the opposing back, provided the opposing back is not lurking more than the fair distance of a full stroke away.

There is a good deal to be said in favor of No. 1 not riding up on the ball at all when it has been ridden over but staying back with his man. But when he does this there is always the chance that the opposing No. 4 will slip past him and steal a march, or that one of the other side will turn first and get to the ball when No. 1 could have been standing over it and kept it away from the first opponent round by passing it conveniently to one of his own side, as before explained. No. 1 has to be guided by circumstances in such cases. If he sees that his No. 2 is going to get round first, his position is back alongside of this man to clear the way for the rush to goal.

Crane says the back should never let his No. 1 come in alone and steal the ball from his No. 3.

From time to time it is well for men who are going to play No. 2 and No. 1 to change places in practice, No. 1 to play No. 2 and No. 2 to play No. 1, for a week or two. Thus each may see the difficulties of the other teammate's position, and No. 1 can get a much better idea of what No. 2 is calling for and why. "As others see us" is a pretty good point of view.

A propos of all No. 1's knowing how to play No. 2, Allan Forbes says: "No, 2's should know how to play No. 1 and be willing to do so; most No. 2's play one and a half." This means that No. 2 too often hangs back and plays about half way between his own position and that of No. 1; in other words, he doesn't stay by the opposing back.

On the knock in by his own side, No. 1's duty is to place himself advantageously near the opposing back and keep him out of the play. Without unduly giving the play away, he should be ready to put himself on that side of the opposing back to which the ball is to be hit and then bother him. I have sometimes placed my pony directly across in front of back and let him extricate himself when the time came to move.

Allan Forbes says that it is often better for the No. 1 to place himself a little off to one side, counting on his man to pass the ball to him, in this way forcing the back to play to cover him.

When the opposing team is knocking in, No. 1 should place himself about thirty yards out, directly in front of the place where experience has shown him that the opposing No. 4 usually hits. If he usually hits to the side, No. 1 should stand on the line from the ball to the side lines; if to the center he should place himself in front of it, toward the center; if at a diagonal, he should place himself diagonally in; but in every case he should ride in to endeavor to meet the ball as it is knocked in. It is his fault if the ball is dribbled and the opposing back comes up and hits it a second time.

No. 1's great chance for a brilliant play is to get away with the ball before the opposing back is ready. His pony should be trained to start instantly to rush at speed on seeing a clear field, for speed is the essence of good polo. No. 1 should realize that the time spent in waiting is just what is needed to save the pony so that he will be fresh when the time has come that speed is needed.

CHAPTER VIII

DUTIES OF No. 2

No. 2's primary duties are to keep himself, as nearly as possible, immediately on or over the ball when on the offensive. He alone of his side should follow the ball into the offensive corners; he must be the fastest and most accurate hitting one on the team. He must not let the opposing No. 3 carry the ball on the defense, and he must not let the opposing No. 3 back it on the offense. Of course, the best way to prevent this is to place oneself in regard to the opposing No. 3 as to get to it first on the offense or defense. There are few chances for No. 2 to save their ponies. He ordinarily must have more ponies than any other man on the team. If No. 3 needs five, No. 2 needs six ponies for his matches. Back can get along very easily with four; No. 1 won't unnecessarily strain three. Of course these figures vary with different players and their manner of playing. I have always thought that No. 2 and No. 3 ought to have particularly handy ponies; that handiness in the center was very important; and if in any given period of a match one of the two gets up on a fast pony that is not handy, the other should be careful to compensate by selecting a handy pony. Of course, with a fast game a slow pony in the center is perfectly hopeless, and is assumed that No. 2 and No. 3 in important matches are well mounted and all their ponies are at least of average speed and not outclassed by the run of ponies playing.

On the throw in, No. 2 should make a special effort to get the ball, being particular at the same time that No. 2 of the opposing side does not get it. Whoever does get the ball, it is No. 2's business immediately to follow up the play. If the opposing No. 3 gets it, it will be No. 3's business to stay with him, No. 2 probably trailing. If his No. 3 gets the ball on the throw in, it is probably that his opposing No. 3 will stay by him, taking temporarily No. 2's place, so that, unless No. 2 has been very quick in starting off ahead, the two No. 2's will be correspondingly placed and will fight it out for the position of supporting.

What is said about supporting from too close under the head of "Duties of No. 1," applies also to No. 2, who must never under any circumstances ride too near to the couples in front of him, as No. 3 is shown to be doing in Fig. 6. If the ball is ridden over and No. 2 is riding fast and too close, he also will ride over it; and if he is riding ahead of his opposing No. 3, whom he has left riding clear, he is committing an unpardonable crime against proper polo. He should always stay back far enough to cover his man. It is his fault if the opposing No. 3 gets the ball. It is his business to see that No. 3 does not get it, and to get it himself. Of course, with two perfect players, which one gets the ball will depend just on how it happens to be hit away or the way the ball is left, whether to one side or the other. But every player should aim to be a player superior to the man opposite him, and he should devote his energies to outmaneuvering his man if he can, placing himself on the opponent's mallet side and a little in advance of his pony in the direction in which the ball and the player are moving. Then he has got what in yachting is called a "weather berth" and is in position to put his opponent out of the play and get the ball himself.

Crane says: "No. 2 should take every chance on the offense and No. 3 should take practically no chance except one stroke from opponent's goal.

No. 2 should, by following the No. 1 and No. 4 at speed, force his opposing No. 3 to play closer to that pair than he otherwise would and thus nullify No. 3's defense. No. 3 cannot afford to let his opposing No. 2 play clear in front even if he is too close to No. 1 and No. 4, for the penalty is too great if No. 2 does not bring off a lucky one."

What I have stated in regard to hitting the ball back to a waiting opponent, under the head of "Duties of No. 1," applies with equal force to No. 2. When, on the defensive, No. 3 and No. 4 may have ridden over the ball and No. 2 rides down on it and finds the opposing No. 3 has pulled back to get his back stroke, No. 2 should never hit it to him. His choice lies, as indicated in the chapter on the duties of No. 1 and shown for him in Fig. 20, between riding past the ball when it has ceased to move, turning and coming back on it, or stopping over it and waiting. If the opposing No. 3 has pulled up, there is no danger from infringement on right of way in doing this, but No. 2 must be very careful that he is not rushed and led into fouling by reason of standing over the ball. No. 2 can then take his time in regard to his measure, either dribbling the ball along slowly—following it up until his No. 3 is in position, then passing it to him—or hitting it short until he can ride over it and leave it for his No. 3 to come along; or, if the worst comes to worst, hitting it as far down as he can, on the chance that his No. 1 will be in position to take it along, rather than giving it up to a player of the opposing side. I used to play a short cross-field stroke to the side on which my No. 1 or No. 3 was riding past; in the latter case No. 3 went up to No. 2's position and received the ball on the pass. This gave us a favorable chance for a run down the field, and we usually so arranged it that the opposing No. 3, who had been waiting for such a move, would have to get into the line of play at an angle which put him at a disadvantage and made it possible for my No. 3, now taking the position of No. 2, to get a good run. I, having passed it out to him, would take up the position next to him and ahead of any possible opponent, making sure that in case of my man missing the ball the opposing No. 2 would not get it.

Where No. 2 backs the ball, he must be especially careful to call "Turn," or its equivalent, because his men ahead cannot be looking over their shoulders all the time to see and can do better work if they can count on hearing.

I have always believed that No. 1 is the player to make goals, and when playing No. 2 I do not try for goals unless I am pretty sure of them. I never try a long shot or a difficult angle shot at goal, and such difficult goals as I may have made have been chance rather than design. When the play is at a difficult angle, I try to put it out directly in front of the posts. When it is a long way out I play an approach shot. It takes four times as much skill to hit a goal from 100 yards as it does at 50 yards and four times as much skill from 50 yards as it does from 25 yards. See Figs. 5, 7, and 8 when No. 2 should try and approach shot first.

I consider it to be a great disadvantage to knock over the back line, and I am always playing to put the ball close in front of the goal posts where another stroke will send it over, rather than relying on any particularly brilliant stroke from a distance.

On the knock in, No. 2 should be at the boards. I like to have it arranged so that when the back knocks the ball in it shall strike the boards, No. 2 placing himself in such a way that he can come down the boards at the point the ball hits and start the rush for the goal at the extreme side of the field, where the danger to one's own goal is at a minimum. By placing himself near the boards, No. 2 will have his opponents lined up for the defense in the field, and if the ball hits the boards it gives a clear shot between the pony and the boards for No. 2 to start his rush. If

No. 2 sees a chance, I see no objection to his cutting or turning the ball out into the field and directly across the line of most of the players who come galloping toward the boards with the ball. This gives him the right of way to himself and often will enable him to come out clear into the field, particularly if No. 1 sees his chance and gets a position between the opposing back and the center of the field. However, I think it safest to bring the ball right along down the side lines, the idea being to get the goal out of danger first. From the sidelines there is less chance of a successful rush toward the defensive goal, if the ball is turned, than from the center. The distance is so great from the goal you are trying to make that the angle is not a sharp one if you straighten it for the goal before getting past the middle of the field.

I consider it the acme of pad polo to send the ball toward the boards at all in the offensive half of the field, unless it is done purposely, as, for example, for the purpose of gaining time, or, as is explained under "Team play," as part of a strategic move to change the line of play.

No. 2 should always bear in mind that the correct line of play is from the center of the ball to the center of the goal line he is trying to make, and every stroke that parallels that line of play establishes a right of way in the direction which is most direct to the opponent's goal and therefore most advantageous. It is his particular job to establish a right of way along that line, but a potential right of way is only good if it is maintained, and the way to that is to get on it and hold it at speed.

To hit straight to goal all the time is a very good rule, care being taken to avoid hitting to opponents who are clear and that can be avoided by the simple device of hitting short, the direction still, if possible, being right straight to goal. An exception to this rule is to be found on page 178, where the advantages of angle hitting are explained at length. (See Figure 25)

When the opponents are knocking in, No. 2 should place himself directly in front of the posts. Or, if the ball has gone out well over toward the side, he can take his place a few feet toward the goal from somewhere between the ball and goal posts and far enough out to stand a chance of intercepting the first stroke. It is No. 2's business to block any attempt to carry the ball round the field or across goal. He waits to get a pass in case the ball is blocked and hit to him by one of his own men, but he must take his position to cover his player the minute the ball is hit. His man in this case may be the opposing back if he is riding through, or it may be No 3, who is probably stationed somewhere near him defending goal. No. 2 should be in position to receive the knock in by riding with the ball. He should be ready, however, to turn immediately in case of a very short stroke on the part of the man who is knocking in. If the ball passes near him it always pays to have a swing at it, but in cross-goal plays he should be very careful in so doing not to lose his position for the defense and let the one who knocked it in get by them and go down the field clear, as their team is depending upon them to prevent that.

To No. 2, as to all other players, I will repeat the admonition that they must ride rapidly until they are in position, after the balls goes outside or at any time, and, once solidly in position, take all the leisure they can.

No. 2 should remember, as should all other players, that the strongest defense is a strong offense—that if he rides his man religiously and conscientiously, keeping in front of the opposing No. 3, whichever way the play is going, playing for the ball when the opportunity arrives, so as to put the other player in the position of doing the riding off, he can really be the mainstay of the team. No. 2 wants to remember that the essence of all polo is hitting straight and true on the off side. If he is really on his job, the play will be fast; if he is not on his job, the play will be slow. In other words, No. 2 is the one on whom the team usually depends for making the game fast.

Where a particularly good chance comes, it is justifiable for No. 2 to cut across the line of the ball and take it around instead of backing it. Provided that his first stroke toward the center will leave him in position to get an easy angle for his second stroke to the goal, this is often preferable to backing it toward the side. That the stroke is more difficult is compensated for by the improved opportunity it offers to carry the ball, and by the fact that the defensive line is intact with his No. 3 and No. 4 in position to defend in case of a miss on his part. No. 2 is, however, more justified in doing it near the opponent's goal than he is near his own goal, where the defense is more important and he should make the surer stroke and where the fact that he is taking it toward the boards is an advantage rather than otherwise.

CHAPTER IX

DUTIES OF No. 3

No. 3 ought to keep over the ball all the time on the defense. He is the first line of defense. If No. 2 is the most aggressive and active player on the field, No. 3 should be the most careful and the most skillful. He should be eternally vigilant. He should combine readiness for whirlwind riding any minute with a feeling that he must be ready to defend goal and play the safe, conservative game of back. He must remember that the strongest defense is a strong offense; that a goal can never be properly defended if the team is not ready to take the offensive on the first move; that he cannot help his back by galloping down on him; that he must never come back and do the back's work for him unless he has first passed the word to the back that has taken his place and back has accepted the change and gone up to take the place of No. 3.

A defensive stroke is practically worthless unless it is followed up by turning it to an offensive movement. There is nothing more hopeless for a team than to have the back strokes constantly met as they are sent down by opponents who are riding clear, particularly when they should be covered. Thus No. 3's business is not only to defend the goal but also to keep the opposing No. 2 out of the play. He must be careful not to leave him as shown in Fig. 6. The opposing No. 2 is apt to be formidable, the most aggressive, fastest, hardest hitting, and most effective player on the opposing team.

If No. 3 gets it into his head that it is his job to ride back and hit splendid back strokes, regardless of whom he is sending them to or where the opposing No. 2 is, he will often play as freely into the hands of the opposing side as though he were actually trying to do so.

At the risk of repetition, then, No. 3's work is not only to support his back, not only to prevent the play from passing him, but so to place himself in relation to the opposing No. 2 that he covers him in so doing. Of course, if No. 2 is playing too far back and pulls up whenever the couple in front have ridden each other over the ball, No. 3 will do what any good player should and what has been indicated to the other players—either stop over the ball or turn on it.

On the throw in, No. 3 has the simplest business of anyone, as well as the most obvious. He rides for the ball, stays with his opposing No. 3 if he gets it, and in so doing he holds his own position. If the ball rolls through and No. 4 gets it, No. 3 follows him up immediately, ready to take the position of No. 4 in case the rush is blocked. If, on the throw in, he gets the ball himself, he of course follows it right through and may by so doing get into No. 2's position, in which case he should say to his No. 2 "I am 2," to which No. 2 replies "I am 3." They continue holding these positions until a good chance comes to change.

In following up a stroke, No. 3 should always lay himself far enough back so that a disarrangement of the play by the ball having hit the stick of his No. 2 or a pony's foot will not cause him to ride over it. His distance back, however, should be regulated by the distance of the opposing No. 2. If he has No. 2 covered so that he cannot get the ball, No. 3's duty is done, and no kick can come if he doesn't get the ball himself. Then if the ball is moving in the offensive direction it is up to No. 4 to be ahead of his man and come through and take it. Similarly, if on the defensive, No. 3 and his corresponding opponent ride over the ball, it is up to No. 2 to be ahead of his man and get the ball.

In any case No. 3 has done his first duty when he has covered his man.

When his side is knocking in, No. 3 should take his place about ten yards south and somewhere between the ball and the goal posts. No. 4 hits the ball and follows it through thus temporarily passing No. 3, unless the team shall prefer to have No. 3 knock in, an equally advantageous play, in my judgment. If there is any check, No. 3 and No. 4 can find their places, passing the word as they pass. No. 3's business is to see that the ball is not met by the opposing No. 1 or some other players and sent through the goal posts. He should take up a position about ten yards in the field and between the point where the ball is placed and the goal post. If the ball went out from near the post he should be directly in front of the goal, and in any case he should place himself in position so as to save goal in case the ball is met or returned before he and No. 4 have resumed places. No. 3 may also line up advantageously between No. 4 and No. 2 as suggested by Crane. (See page 77.)

When the opponents are knocking in, No. 3's business is near the boards to stop No. 2 getting the ball and carrying it down.

What I have said in other places in regard to the carrying of the ball round has particular force in its application to the position of No. 3. No. 3 should hit to his own players, not to himself

He should back the ball in the line it is traveling and send it almost directly back, selecting such little deflection to the side as he can safely make, so as to hit it clear of the nearest opposing player and his pony or toward where one of his own side is waiting.

Although it is particularly vicious for No. 3 to take the ball around, there is always the exception if the ball is traveling at an angle with the goal line he is defending and he gets a particularly good chance at turning on it, and, in turning it, he is hitting in a general direction toward the goal he is trying to make, not leaving for himself a difficult angle on his next stroke or riding in a great circle which the opponents can cut across to block him at any point, it is sometimes justifiable for him to turn the ball. This is only justifiable as an offensive play when near the opponents' goal or in defending when the cross-field stroke will send the ball clearly ahead and well across the field. It should never be played at the risk of making a safety.

No. 3 should always remember that players following can spoil a forward stroke by hooking when a back stroke can be safely got off. He should be absolutely sure he is taking no chance of getting caught this way if he tries to carry it ahead.

No. 3 and No. 4 are two men on the team who can hit long strokes with impunity, and No. 3 should make a particular effort to get his back strokes long. There is nothing that reflects itself quicker on the change from offense to defense than a long back stroke. Players of the same side get to expect it and turn it rapidly to account. In the desire to secure distance, the greatest care should be taken not to sacrifice the certainty of hitting, as that is one of the most important parts of No. 3's play and one of the things most to be taken into account in selecting a player for the position.

Crane adds: "Protect your back at all costs and feed the ball up to your No. 1 and No. 2. Change with your back often to throw opposing No. 1 out and to equalize more with physical strain. Always change with No. 2 where time can be saved. If back is turned upon your back stroke, don't turn until you are sure the ball has started up, then play conservatively back to give your No. 4 confidence to change places with you."

In summing up my directions to No. 3, I should say, "Be vigilant! vigilant! vigilant!"

CHAPTER X

DUTIES OF No. 4

No. 4 or back is the defensive man on the team and the court of last resort. He should learn to have timidity in regard to his goal line that renders him apprehensive of every possible move against it. He should be cautious about playing close up to the line.

Crane remarks: "It is safer to be close up as long as back has the opposing No. 1 securely covered than to be back a part of a stroke." He makes the general comment that a back should stay as close in as is safe and be alert to turn either way.

By playing deeper he can usually accomplish more than he can by riding in and toying with fire. When I say playing deeper, I do not mean from more than thirty or forty yards away, according to the speed of the play. These distances may be shortened somewhat as the opponent's goal is neared, in order that he may be in position to rush through and make a goal, but No. 4 must remember that, however brilliant his rushes may be, however strong he may be in getting through on the offensive occasionally, his job is to defend the goal, and his stunt is turning the ball back whenever it gets started toward his goal and passes No. 3. More backs make mistakes by playing close up to their lines and coming to charge than by staying far back. In the main, the back must remember that if he has played his defense well he has played his game well.

No. 4 should be a successful maneuverer, who ought to be watching all the time to see how the opposing No. 1 is staking up—what sort of position he is making for himself. No. 4 should be very adroit at getting the opposing No. 1 started fast and then pulling up and clearing him. He should be watching all the time to keep the opposing No. 1, if possible, on the near-side so as to have his own mallet side clear. It is occasionally justifiable for No. 4 to meet the ball where he is perfectly sure he is going to hit it, or where he sees that No. 3 is in a favorable position to get it in case he misses it, in which case No. 4 should pass the word to No. 3 to take the defensive position. Under the head of "Match playing" I have discussed the strategy of changing the whole style of playing the last few moments of a match when the game is otherwise hopelessly lost.

On the throw in, No. 4 should line up a few yards off half way between the positions of No. 2 and No. 3. As the ball rolls back and looks as though it were going to pass through the opposing couples, he should swing his pony gradually until the ball passes the last couple, when he should dash in and try to get the ball for a rush to goal. If the opposing No. 4 is similarly alert in making the rush, they will have to guard mutually against collision, but it is No. 4's job either to get it or to prevent the other No. 4 from getting it. If, on the throw in, any of the opponents get the ball, No. 4 should immediately start back to defend.

The essence of No. 4's job is to back the ball, as is carefully explained in the chapter on "Use of the mallet," swinging his mallet along the line the ball is traveling for certainty in hitting and always taking care to see where the rush of oncoming ponies is and to send the ball where it will not be hit by ponies or players as they come. It is easier to hit to the left than to the right, as it is easier to draw the stroke across behind the pony than to make the cut stroke to deflect it. When he has time, No. 4 should wait until he is well past the ball before hitting it so as to get the full force of the swing and not to knock it into the ground. But he must take due care not to pass too far so as to send the ball too high in air, as that is more likely to be stopped and, besides, loses distance.

No. 4 should never cut across the line of the ball in trying to save goal, unless the ball has stopped moving. In this case he has an equally good chance for any direction if he can cross the line the ball has been traveling without fouling, and, in case of a forward stroke, be sure of not being hooked. He should remember that, more than anything else, his job is to hit the ball and hit it true. More depends upon his stroke than upon that of any other player, and he must not try fancy strokes when a plain one will do the work as well or better. His job is not a spectacular one—it is a safe one.

On the knock in, No. 4 usually hits the first stroke. He is relied upon to hit a long stroke, and he should try to have the ball strike the boards every time. If he feels he cannot send it to the boards, either because the ball is too near the goal posts or because he is not a strong enough or sure enough hitter, he should hit the ball as near along the back line as he can, following it fast and hitting the second stroke to the boards.

Under no circumstances should No. 4 hit the ball directly out in front of the posts. If there is a signal for cross-goal hitting, No. 4 should hit well across, so that the ball will get well toward the boards of the other side; but he should never send the ball straight down the field with the expectation of hitting it a second time. The balance of chance is all against the side that makes this flash play. I have seen more goals lost by silly hitting out toward the center, when the ball could just as well have gone toward the side lines, than from any other one unnecessary and foolish misplay. Play safe, and safety demands that the ball be not knocked in front of the goal you are defending. The turf in front of the goal posts, for one thing, is cut up more than at any other part, as it gets the most wear, and the ball is less likely to travel true and is more likely to bounce here than in any other part of the territory adjacent to the end lines.

When the opposing side is knocking in, No. 4 should take his position as the second defense, expecting No. 3 to get the first stroke at the ball and send it back. No. 4 should be placed nearer the center of the field than No. 3 and not very far away, and should not meet the ball unless the ball has already stopped or his stroke is absolutely certain, or unless No. 3 has got past him and is taking his defensive position.

On the offensive, the back should place himself in such a way as to back up his No. 3 and No. 2 and to be ahead of the opposing No. 1 in a rush for the opponent's goal.

In case his No. 1, No. 2 and No. 3 ride over the ball and No. 4 is next, he, of course, comes through, calling "Go on" to his side.

If the opposing No. 1, however has him covered so that he cannot get through to hit the ball, No. 4 must then call "Turn" or its equivalent, pull up, and watch for his own side to get round. If he sees his No. 3 is well in position to defend, he can rush the opposing No. 1 to prevent his having time to turn or pass the ball, but in such case he should call to No. 3 to go back and protect goal.

Crane says that No. 4 should always rush the opposing No. 1 if his No. 3 is around first.

I have seen beginners, when told to go back, think it meant necessarily to pull up and go to some place behind them, when in reality they were heading back and all they needed was to whip up and go ahead. No. 3 and No. 4 should understand clearly what

"Back" means. It means to go toward the defensive goal. It means playing a deeper defensive, so if they are heading back, a signal to go back indicates that they must go ahead fast.

No. 4 should always be looking for a chance to get through with the ball. The most brilliant backs I have known have been those who, when a chance came for a rush, came crashing through at high speed, being in a better position to get up high speed because their ponies have less rushing and turning to do and are therefore fresher.

When he comes through this way, back should be particularly careful to call "Go on" to his men, as his rush is not the expected thing, his job being to play the defensive, and his own players will not necessarily expect him to come through unless they are informed that he is doing it. Having rushed up into the game, back should be very careful to pass the word to No. 3, so that No. 3 will assume his responsibilities, and No. 3 should play religiously back, preferably fairly deep, and stay there until the opportunity comes to change to his own place. When the ball turns direction, or when it is taken round the field there is usually a favorable opportunity to regain position.

In summing up No. 4's job, I should say "Sure, careful, deep, resourceful, and always safe, very safe."

CHAPTER XI

DUTIES OF THE CLUB MANAGER

It is the duty of the manager of the club to see that all players get their share of polo. He or she should be most scrupulous in encouraging the poorer players and beginners. There is always the necessity of steering between the difficulty, on the one hand, of depriving everybody of fast polo by giving the poorer players equal chance with the better ones, and, on the other hand, the difficulty of discouraging the poorer players and beginners by not giving them their money's worth and the opportunity to play often enough. The manager should be very resourceful to overcome these difficulties—for example, by getting the better players out early, so that they may have a few periods before the others come or so grouping the teams as to let the poorer players play for certain periods and the better players play in others. One thing should be borne in mind always, and that is that the strength of a polo club as a club lies not in the strength of its best three or four players, but in the strength of the average player; that if a manager builds all their hopes upon the club's best players and sacrifices to their development and welfare the interests of others, he or she is sacrificing the interests of the club. The continued playing of any one set of players is uncertain. If the club gets dependent on them, when they go out the club is lost, whereas, if the manager adopts the policy of developing the best qualities of each new player and encouraging them by giving every opportunity, there will be a crop of players—ready to step into the place of any player going out—who will very shortly become good players, just by reason of the fact that they are to play on the team. My experience has been that with the proper opportunity and coaching, play may be rounded out very rapidly. When I was coaching the university football team at Harvard, I almost preferred to begin a new season with new material than to have too much of the old. It never discouraged me to put in a new man. Start the players right and the responsibility of playing a team game with a team that has won its spurs will prove to be an incentive to almost any player that will result in them molding themselves within an almost incredibly short period of time. The fact that there are experienced players before and behind enables the player to find position very much more rapidly than if left to their own devices floundering about in the chaos of a beginner's polo game.

Where the polo squad is twelve or less, there should be an agreement among the players to give up all minor engagements and present themselves at the field in time to make a game so that five or six players will not be kept waiting until some belated one or two arrive. The club manager should endeavor to stimulate among the players a spirit that will make them alive to their responsibilities in this respect.

Players should be given opportunities to play in direct proportion to the number of ponies they have. The one-pony player is entitled to one period in three; a two-pony player is expected to drop out much oftener than a three-pony player,, while a player who maintains four or more ponies should play right along and get cut out of play only one or two periods in an afternoon.

Where more than twelve are out, I have found that it pays to arrange three teams, each a different color—red, yellow, and blue. The Reds and Yellows play one period and then the Reds and Blues have a period; the Reds thus play twice in succession. The Red team then goes out and the Yellows and Blues have a turn.

Where there are more than fifteen players, four teams can be formed and no intervals allowed, as when the first two teams to play ride off the field, two more teams ride on and thus the maximum of playing is provided. In the case of players with only one pony, adjustments can be made by substituting the players with several in their places. Although this makes a constant shifting of the personnel of most of the teams, it is advisable except in preparing for matches. Then the players that are to be played as teams should be kept as much as possible together and the changes made in other groups of players.

Where there are great numbers, the hours of play should be longer, so as to give everybody a chance to go in. Where the players are few, the hours of play should be shorter and the intervals longer. Where a player for any reason wants to stay out, he or she should give notice to the captain immediately on dismounting, not, as usually seems to be the practice, just as the teams are mounting to get into place. I believe it advisable to have a little painted tin slips, with the names of the players, which can be placed in a rack where all can see. The manager, having selected the Blue team, sets up their names and positions on the Blue rack. The club manager should designate the captain of the team as they go out. The Red team should be on the Red rack and the captain designated. Now that we do much of communication via the internet and email it makes the signing up for chukkers and the sending out of rosters in advance of play a much easier task. Most clubs now have on line systems in place to sign up for and receive confirmation of weekly practice chukkers and game schedules. As soon as the bell rings practice should start, and there should always be an umpire or referee— one of the players, or some person on horseback—to throw in the ball and start the play. Before any line up is called, about ten minutes should be devoted to limbering up and getting the ponies worked for a few minutes and the strokes steadied.

For this warming up, it is best to have the goal posts moved fifteen or twenty yards toward the side of the field in order that the concentration of ponies at the goal may not tear up the field in the center of the goal, thus saving the turf between and about the goal posts. If this practice is pursued the goal line itself will be infinitely less cut up, as in an hour or two of actual play there will not be more than fifteen or twenty goals made—say, eight at each end. In the practice beforehand, there are likely to be forty at each end in ten minutes. During non-practice chukkers and daily stick and ball it is also helpful to avoid a constant back and forth on the field between goals taking shots at each approach to goal for the same reason of saving the field. Better when working at stick and ball practice to move in circles, use the sides of the field and angles to practice both with hitting the ball and working the horses.

It is proper to let the poorer players and beginners have the less important posts in the team play in practice. A new man should go to No. 1 until he earns the right to move into the somewhat more responsible positions. Unless developing a player for some particular and immediate purpose, I put my strongest men in the position of No. 2 and No. 3 and put their weaker players at the ends.

Colors should be ready and strapped onto the players as they start to play, and the manager or a designee should be on hand to see that each player has their colors off before leaving the field. If this is not done, the players will wear them away as sure as fate and often forget to bring them back, so that the club will constantly have to supply new colors.

CHAPTER XII

DUTIES OF THE TEAM CAPTAIN

The team captain is charged with the conduct of the game and the direction of the play.

The most important part of his duty is to make sure that his men are holding their positions. If play is going badly against his team, he should be able to size up the reason for it. More than likely it is the fault of some one player. Not long ago I was playing on a team that by all rules should have been very strong and should have easily beaten its competitors, but it didn't. I got worried and began analyzing the reason for it, watching each player with the greatest solicitude, but for some days I failed to detect the weakness till by the process of elimination it gradually came to me that the weak place was at No. 2, the position I was playing. I then got busy and began looking less for faults in others. Some men get a fancy in their heads that they can help by going back and helping another of their own side. That is most likely to be the case when the game is going against them and No. 2 or No. 3 get it into their heads that they can help No. 4 by going back and making his back strokes for him. If here is anything that kills a team, it is that. The best way they can help No. 4 is by holding their positions and making the advance effective when the time comes to take the ball ahead. The captain should see that players hold their position, even if the game is going against them, cover their man, and be sure to let the fault lie with some other player, if fault there be, and not add to it by turning the whole game into hopeless confusion by leaving their posts to do somebody else's work. The fact is, no player can do anybody else's work, and with one position uncovered the team is crippled.

The captain should be most scrupulously careful not to blame other men for his own misplay. If he does, he wills soon lose his influence with the team and the spirit of the team will go to pieces. No player finds fault with a just criticism, even when expressed in extremely forcible language. Even though sore for a few moments, when he comes to think it over and sees that he is to blame, he comes back chastened in spirit and bearing no ill feeling. Polo is not a game where you can stop and say "Please." The orders of the captain must be sharp, immediate, and peremptory, and instantly obeyed by his players.

The captain should remember that no man can play well with constant criticism. All players must be encouraged. Anyone will go to pieces if the only words that come from the lips of a captain are those of blame. Every encouraging symptom should be noted, and praise should be given wherever praise is due and in equal measure to the blame.

The captain should make sure that the men do those simple things so necessary for their proper playing which are carelessly left out by a great many players. He should tell them to feel their mallet heads before mounting for each period in a match. He should stir them up to be ready on time. He should insist upon quick lining up, each man taking his place when the ball goes out. He should train each player so that, when the ball goes out of bounds he will gallop rapidly to his position as though the play were still in process and then stop and get his wind after his is in place, not before. Nearly two-thirds of the players I have seen have the fault of pulling up and taking too much time getting into position after the ball goes outside, with the result that they are reaching their position when the ball is thrown or knocked out, instead of being in it. If the referee or knocker-in is at all expeditious, a quick man can take advantage of this carelessness of his opponents to be on hand and get the ball a great many times when a little promptness on the part of the opposing players would have prevented it.

It is the captain's business before the game to toss up for choice of sides. In choosing sides he should take into account sun and wind. It is easier to play down the wind than against it, and if it happens that the field lies so that the sun is in the eyes, that might offset a head wind and make is wise to choose the side with the back to the sun.

The captain should allow no talking back on the field by the players. In the main, talking on the field by the players should be confined to the words which I have indicated under the head of "Team play," which amount to keeping your side informed as to what is going on, but the captain of the team should speak and coach the other players. A team will listen to the orders or criticisms of the captain, whose business it is to talk, but ill spirit results if all players undertake to coach or find fault with each other. I do not, however, mean to preclude old experienced players sending new men back to their places, if they come in to crowd them or get out of place. In fact, any player who gets out of place must expect to hear of it very sharply. There is no way a man can be trained to learn his place except by a man whose territory is invaded letting him know he is out of place, and nobody can blame him if it is a fairly sharp reminder. The captain should be particularly careful never to scold the player for having done badly if his intention were right that is, if he misses a stroke or does not get his pony pulled up and turned fast enough to cover some other player or players, especially if called upon to ride an extremely good horseman or man on a particularly fast pony, o, in other words, where he has done practically everything that he ought but did not do it quite well enough. Vituperations in such cases will only do harm, and the player scolded will be discouraged, not helped. If he has turned in a circle instead of pulling up in his tracks and turning, that is an incorrect play; he should have known better and should be roundly brought to task. Or if he has failed to ride off or crook the other man's stick, letting him have a free swing when he could have prevented it, or if he has begun his stroke at the ground and ridden past the ball before his mallet got around, the captain should very properly call his attention sharply to his error.

In selecting the teams it is well to bear in mind the following facts:

Of an average sixteen strokes,

No. 2 will hit six

No. 3 will hit five

No. 4 will hit three

No. 1 will hit two.

It is No. 2's position to be on the ball at the time on the offensive, and No. 3's to be on the ball on the defensive, and, as a natural result, they get most of the hitting. Thus, on the general theory of chance, as No. 2 is in position where most of the hitting comes naturally, the most accurate hitter should be selected for the position. I believe that, except for special circumstances, a team will be strongest if its best player is at No. 2, its next best at No. 3, its next best at No. 4, and the poorest at No. 1, which is the position in which a poor player can do the least harm. The position of No. 1 has very naturally come to be looked down upon. In view of the foregoing it is almost paradoxical to say that it is the position where the best player can do the most good, and I have been accustomed to measure the strength of strong teams by their No. 1. In the great international championship game of 1909 won by American in England, L. Waterbury supposed to be the best player on the American team, was placed in the position of No. 1. This seems to be inconsistent with my general theory of play, but, given a team where No. 2 and No. 3 are sufficiently able to cover their positions and do it on equal terms with the No. 2 and NO. 3 of the opposing side, the strength in the position of No. 1 is what a business man would call "velvet," and means goal after goal.

Crane comments that if the team is winning, No. 2 will hit oftener, but if the team is losing and generally on the defense, No. 3 will have more strokes.

I believe, however, that in average play No. 2 will get the most shots; they hit more short ones, for one thing. I advise selecting the team on the assumption that you are going to win.

Crane makes the following comment in regard to most important qualifications: "No. 1 should be deadly on goal and quick to act on his chances. No. 2 should be as sure as possible of goal and the most dashing, active man and chance taker. No. 3 should be a good strong hitter both ways on both sides and safe and sure at backing up No. 2 or at back. No. 4 should be a strong back-hand hitter on both sides and conservative. No. 2 and No. 3 should be very handy."

In preparing a team for its matches, a captain should not call on his men for supreme and unusual efforts. They are usually nervous and pitched to high tension, and need soothing and confidence rather than stimulation. Some few men are so phlegmatic that they need to be urged, but it is seldom or never that a team, as a team, needs such treatment.

The first thing a team needs is confidence. Captains should try to see that the players are confident that good team play is going to win against superior individual play. I have, as captain, very often told my men that, if the score was not more than three goals against us in the first three periods, we were sure to win, doing this in the belief that brilliant playing is apt to tire itself and get worn down by cooperative play on the part of four steady and quiet players, and because the expectation on the part of one team that the other side was going to show a kind of flash in the pan tends to give them confidence against an adverse score which they would not have otherwise. I have often noticed this to be the case.

I also tell my men to meet a rush with a rush, and, if their side is pressed very hard, to grit their teeth and come back hard at their opponents.

CHAPTER XIII

MATCH PLAYING

Preparation for matches should be much more careful than for practice, and there are certain precautions which is pays to take.

In the first place, six, preferably ten, mallets satisfactory to the player should be secured. The player should select their best stick and then get the other ones in the order which they would prefer to use them and give the second best stick to somebody who will agree to stand right at the side lines to deliver the stick in case of necessity. Careful instructions should be given to see that the person holding the mallet does not step on the field in delivering it, as that would be a foul. In very important matches, I should recommend that each team have six people stationed at various points—three on each side of the field, one at the center, and two on either side toward the ends—each with one mallet for each of the four players of the team. Thus, upon losing a stick, a player could gallop to the nearest point and not lose time. It is well to have distinguishing marks on the sticks. I prefer to paint rings around the mallet head or even have the entire head painted in a specific color. By having all of one's mallets in distinguishing colors, you can always tell your own sticks and not by any chance get anybody else's. Initials painted on the head of the mallet are also helpful for this.

Before mounting, the ponies should be selected and orders given to the groom as to the exact order in which they are to be played. Upon mounting one pony, the groom should immediately have the next pony girthed up and ready to go out on a second's notice, so that in case of the breaking of a curb chain or of a stirrup, or some other accident to the pony, the next pony may be mounted without loss of time, as time is golden. Each pony to be ridden in the match should be mounted once before the play to make sure that the stirrups are just right, but it is not necessary to ride them before playing, although it improves some of them to do so. If there is any pony that is particularly fractious and high strung, it is often well to let her have several miles at slow gallop before the play to bring her within the bounds of reason. Two or three miles will steady a pony immensely and not detract from her staying power.

I have found it useful at the beginning of play to take a sponge and moisten the breeches inside the knees and legs so as to assure the grip. By the time the trousers and saddle are seated through, the grip will be first rate, but before that there will have to be a time when the saddle is slippery, and, particularly on near-side strokes, there is a little loss in efficiency.

At the beginning of each period of play, the players should be sure to test their mallet heads and make sure that the mallet has not begun to spring or the head to twist. If there is the least indication of weakness, the mallet should be changed, as, once begun, the stick gives very rapidly, and there is nothing more fatal to direction than a twist in a mallet head.

Always mount your pony before the one-minute bell rings and be in your place waiting for the thirty second bell to ring. Never wait, before getting your position, until that bell has rung. When the thirty second bell rings, begin to count slowly so as to see if you can guess approximately when the ball will be thrown in, all the time watching carefully the hand of the referee. When you think the ball is about to be thrown in, move your pony, so as to get the advantage at the instant the referee puts up his hand and the ball is thrown. When the ball is thrown, you should be moving toward it. As a general rule, the team that wins the throw in usually gets the goal.

In selecting the ponies for the match, it is well for the players to have an understanding so that they will know what ponies the other players on their side will use. If players are trying new ponies or ponies that have particular characteristics, it is well to make the characteristics fit one into the other. For instance, if one player has a particularly handy pony and the other player has one that is fast but not handy, it is well, say, for No. 3 to arrange to ride his handy pony in the period when No. 2 is riding an unhandy pony, to offset the disadvantage. A team should be careful that they don't all get mounted on their poorest ponies at once; this might cripple their efficiency and lose the game just by reason of inability to prevent the other team scoring at will for one period. I have seen this happen more than once, and several times I have seen very bad effects from lack of coordination as to mounts.

Sometimes a team has to arrange the order of its mounts to meet peculiarities in the mounts of the opposing team, but this happens much less often than adjustments of the mounts to fit in with one's own side.

Players, before beginning a match, should go out and get their stroke true, beginning slowly, but being perfectly sure to hit with the center of the stick, and then gradually increase the speed until the stroke comes right. There is no need of continuing after a succession of strokes has indicated that the eye and hand are true.

In preparing for matches, keep to the ponies that are to be played in the matches and do not try new ponies or difficult ones that are not going to playing the games. It unsettles the stroke and accomplishes no useful purpose.

In preparing for a match, it is well to eat a hearty breakfast, indulging in the usual pursuits during the morning, take a light luncheon of some well-cooked and simple food, ending at least two hours before the game is to begin, and taking particular care to be properly hydrated.

Personally, I prefer to have a set of players who are nervous before important matches than players who are not; it is apt to keep them up at their best. If a player is not nervous before an important game, it is apt to be an indication that there is something the matter with them.

When, for any reason, it is desired to delay the play, my practice is to get the ball going slow along the side boards and then stop over it, in so far as can be done without violation of the rules, sending it short distances along the boards, or, if in the field, toward the side or into the corner. It never pays to try to delay the game, however, if you have a good offensive movement under way. Keep the rush going until you are apt to lose the ball, when sometimes it can be turned and sent into the far corners where there is less enthusiasm on the part of the opponents in following and where they cannot do much harm whichever way they hit it. A team may want to delay the game when a player has left the team to change their mallet, or when the game is drawing toward the end and with a victory well in hand and the ponies are tiring or are needed later for further hard work. I always try to save my ponies all I can. It is not right to delay the game by not hitting in on a knock in, or by any violation of rule.

If the game has gone against you and you have one or two goals to make, and only a little while in which to do it, the whole strategy of polo changes. The back should no longer play safe, as there is everything to lose and nothing to gain by doing it. Difficult strokes should be tried in place of easy ones, and the whole team should endeavor to meet the ball at all places and at any angle. A possible victory may be gained by unexpectedly meeting the ball, a change in policy which will surprise and perhaps demoralize the opposing team and make the difference between winning or losing the game.

DIAGRAMS

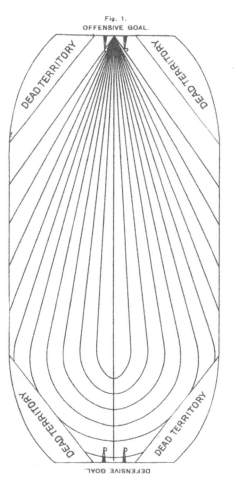

Fig. 1.
OFFENSIVE GOAL.

The lines drawn on this field represent the proper lines for the ball to travel. Any ball which cuts these lines is not effective polo. Every ball which parallels these lines is correct polo. The dead territory is that from which a ball shot at the goal has a reasonable certainty of not going through between the posts. Note: There are exceptions noted in the text when strokes cutting these lines are advantageous.

Fig. 2.

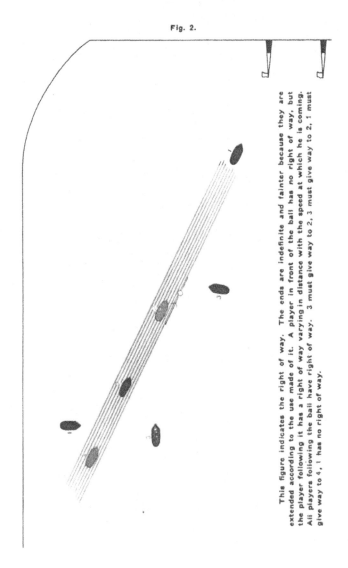

This figure indicates the right of way. The ends are indefinite and fainter because they are extended according to the use made of it. A player in front of the ball has no right of way, but the player following it has a right of way varying in distance with the speed at which he is coming. All players following the ball have right of way. 3 must give way to 2, 3 must give way to 2, 1 must give way to 4, 1 has no right of way.

Fig. 3.

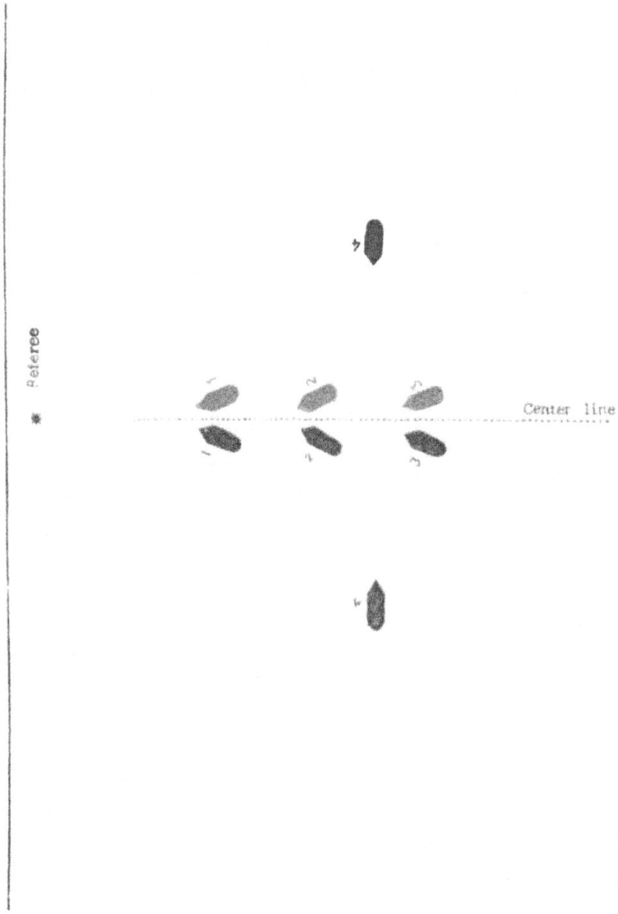

Referee

Center line

The throw in

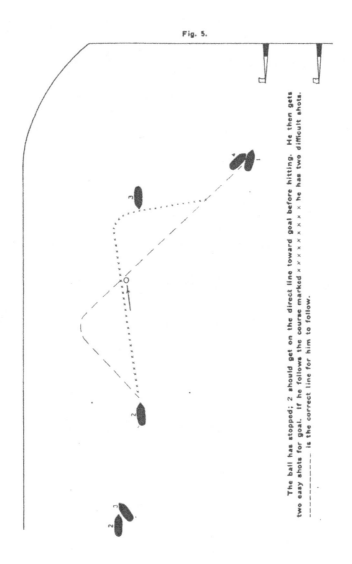

Fig. 5.

The ball has stopped; 2 should get on the direct line toward goal before hitting. He then gets two easy shots for goal. If he follows the course marked × × × × × × × × × × he has two difficult shots. –––––––– is the correct line for him to follow.

Fig. 6.

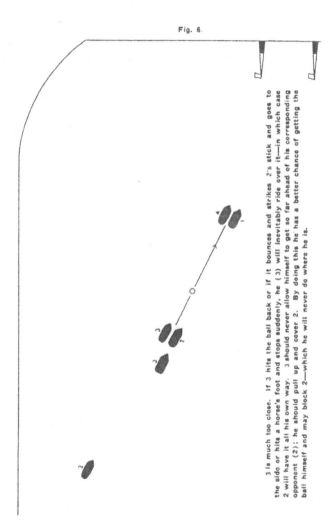

3 is much too close. If 3 hits the ball back or if it bounces and strikes 2's stick and goes to the side or hits a horse's foot and stops suddenly, he (3) will inevitably ride over it—in which case 2 will have it all his own way. 3 should never allow himself to get so far ahead of his corresponding opponent (2); he should pull up and cover 2. By doing this he has a better chance of getting the ball himself and may block 2—which he will never do where he is.

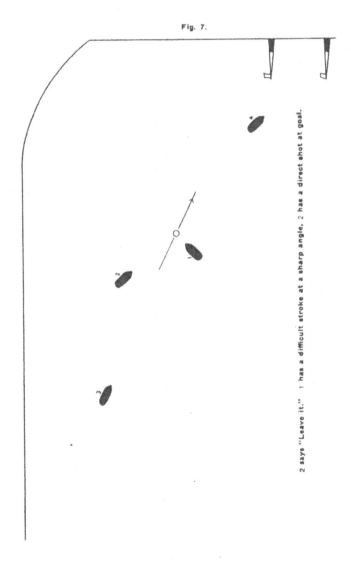

Fig. 7.

2 says "Leave it." 1 has a difficult stroke at a sharp angle, 2 has a direct shot at goal.

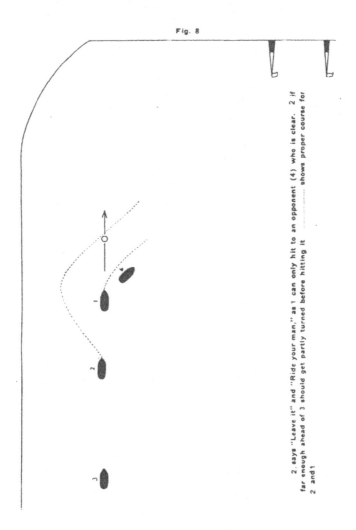

Fig. 8

2 says "Leave it" and "Ride your man," as 1 can only hit to an opponent (4) who is clear. 2 if far enough ahead of 3 should get partly turned before hitting it .... shows proper course for 2 and 1

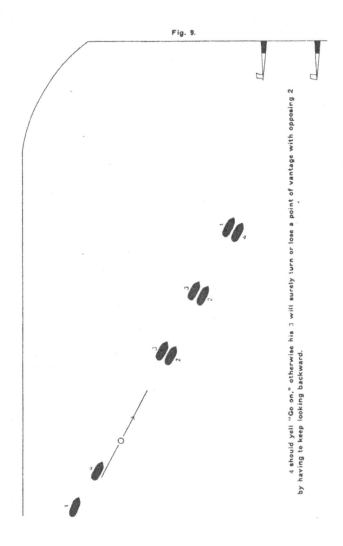

Fig. 9.

4 should yell "Go on," otherwise his 3 will surely turn or lose a point of vantage with opposing 2 by having to keep looking backward.

Fig. 10

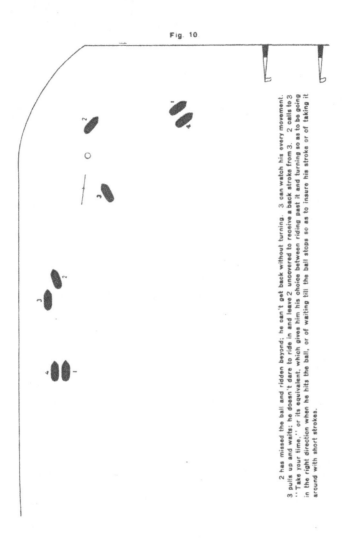

2 has missed the ball and ridden beyond; he can't get back without turning. 3 can watch his every movement. 3 pulls up and waits; he doesn't dare to ride in and leave 2 uncovered to receive a back stroke from 3. 2 calls to 3 "Take your time," or its equivalent, which gives him his choice between riding past it and turning so as to be going in the right direction when he hits the ball, or of waiting till the ball stops so as to insure his stroke or of taking it around with short strokes.

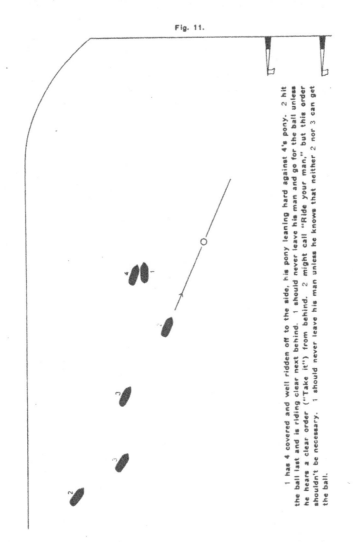

Fig. 11.

1 has 4 covered and well ridden off to the side, his pony leaning hard against 4's pony. 2 hit the ball last and is riding clear next behind. 1 should never leave his man and go for the ball unless he hears a clear order ("Take it") from behind. 2 might call "Ride your man," but this order shouldn't be necessary. 1 should never leave his man unless he knows that neither 2 nor 3 can get the ball.

140

Fig. 12.

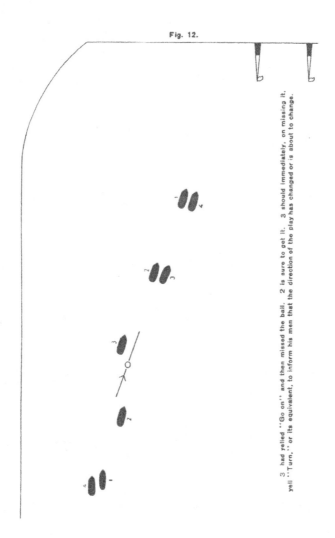

3 had yelled "Go on" and then missed the ball. 2 is sure to get it. 3 should immediately, on missing it, yell "Turn," or its equivalent, to inform his men that the direction of the play has changed or is about to change.

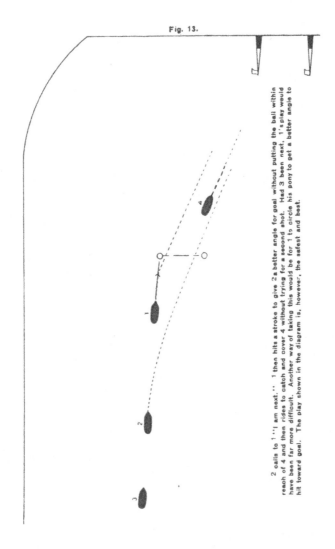

Fig. 13.

2 calls to 1 "I am next." 1 then hits a stroke to give 2 a better angle for goal without putting the ball within reach of 4 and then rides to catch and cover 4 without trying for a second shot. Had 3 been next, 1's play would have been far more difficult. Another way of taking this would be for 1 to circle his pony to get a better angle to hit toward goal. The play shown in the diagram is, however, the safest and best.

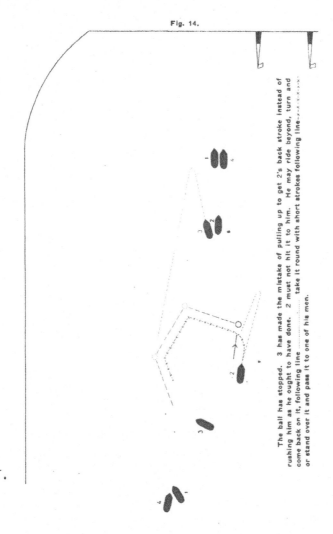

Fig. 14.

The ball has stopped. 3 has made the mistake of pulling up to get 2's back stroke instead of rushing him as he ought to have done. 2 must not hit it to him. He may ride beyond, turn and come back on it, following line .... take it round with short strokes following line–x–x–x–x– or stand over it and pass it to one of his men.

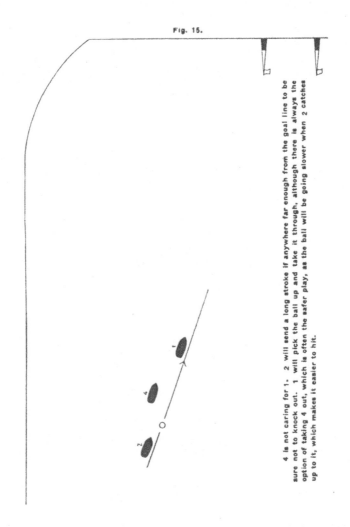

Fig. 15.

4 is not caring for 1. 2 will send a long stroke if anywhere far enough from the goal line to be sure not to knock out. 1 will pick the ball up and take it through, although there is always the option of taking 4 out, which is often the safer play, as the ball will be going slower when 2 catches up to it, which makes it easier to hit.

Fig. 16.

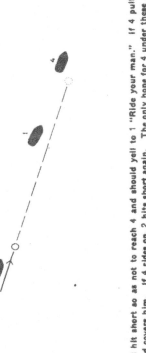

2 should hit short so as not to reach 4 and should yell to 1 "Ride your man." If 4 pulls up, 1 catches up and covers him. If 4 rides on, 2 hits short again. The only hope for 4 under these circumstances is that 3 will catch up and ride 2.

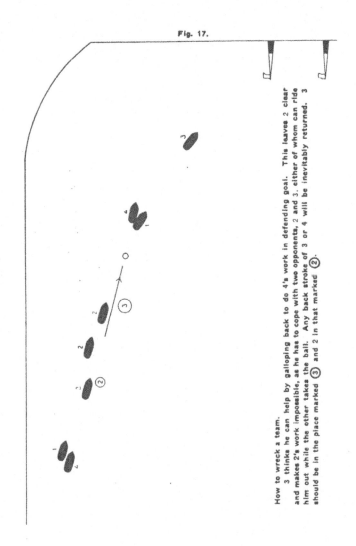

Fig. 17.

How to wreck a team.

3 thinks he can help by galloping back to do 4's work in defending goal. This leaves 2 clear and makes 2's work impossible, as he has to cope with two opponents, 2 and 3, either of whom can ride him out while the other takes the ball. Any back stroke of 3 or 4 will be inevitably returned. 3 should be in the place marked ③ and 2 in that marked ②.

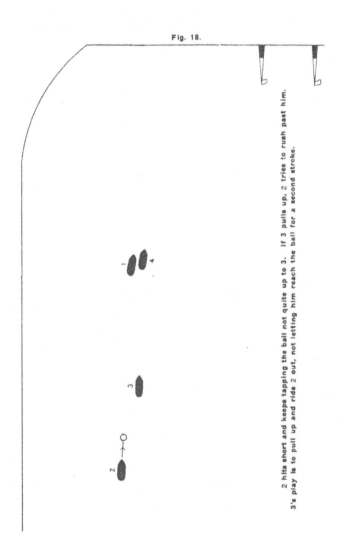

Fig. 18.

2 hits short and keeps tapping the ball not quite up to 3. If 3 pulls up, 2 tries to rush past him. 3's play is to pull up and ride 2 out, not letting him reach the ball for a second stroke.

147

As To Polo

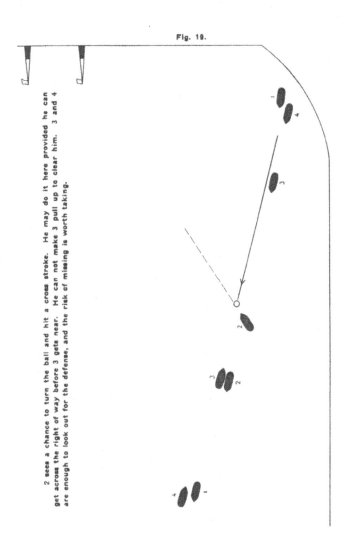

Fig. 19.

2 sees a chance to turn the ball and hit a cross stroke. He may do it here provided he can get across the right of way before 3 gets near. He can not make 3 pull up to clear him. 3 and 4 are enough to look out for the defense, and the risk of missing is worth taking.

148

Fig. 20.

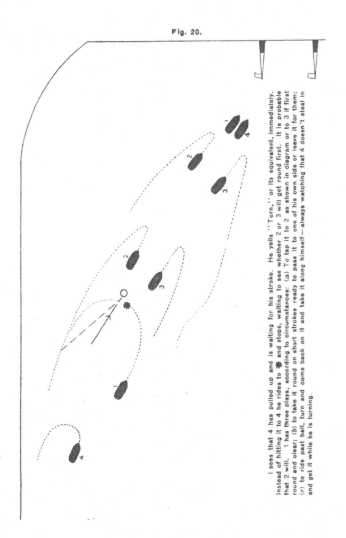

1 sees that 4 has pulled up and is waiting for his stroke. He yells "Turn," or its equivalent, immediately. Instead of hitting it to 4 he rides to ✳ and stops, waiting to see whether 2 or 3 will get round first. It is probable that 2 will. 1 has three plays, according to circumstances: (a) To tap it to 2 as shown in diagram or to 3 if first round and clear; (b) to take it round on short strokes ready to pass it to one of his own side or leave it for them; (c) to ride past ball, turn and come back on it and take it along himself—always watching that 4 doesn't steal in and get it while he is turning.

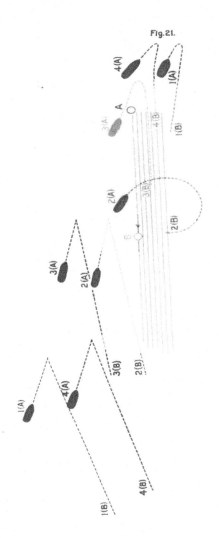

Fig. 21.

The Vicious Circle. A refers to first position of each man and of the ball. B refers to the second position of each. —— Refers to the new right of way. 2 turns in a circle instead of pulling up and turning directly back as do the rest of both teams; 1 and 4 are paired, as are 2 and 3. 3 backs the ball and turns properly, coming down the right of way. Had 2 turned properly he would probably have got the ball, or at least blocked 3. As it is, he is at a hopeless disadvantage and can not interfere with 3 and can barely get round and into place when 4 and 1 come along.

Fig. 22.

The ball is driven into an offensive corner. 2 only goes in after it. 1, 3, and 4 take up position on the edge of live territory to pick up the ball when sent out by 2. 3 rides in for the defense.

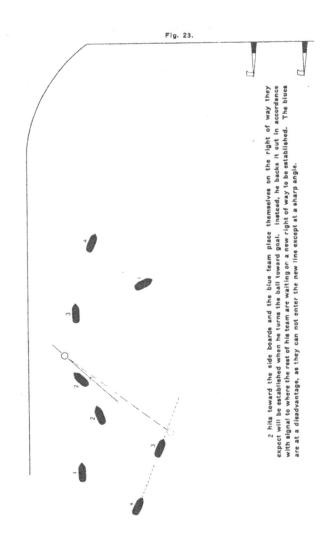

Fig. 23.

2 hits toward the side boards and the blue team place themselves on the right of way they expect will be established when he turns the ball toward goal. Instead, he backs it out in accordance with signal to where the rest of his team are waiting or a new right of way to be established. The blues are at a disadvantage, as they can not enter the new line except at a sharp angle.

Fig. 24.

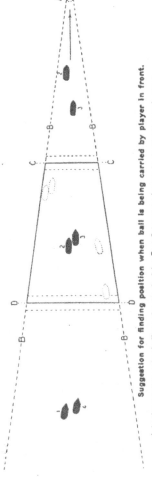

Suggestion for finding position when ball is being carried by player in front.

A is the nearest point ball can be reached by 3 or 2 in case players in front miss or leave it.

BB and BB are drawn at the greatest angle at which a player can ride his pony safely at speed into a pony at A which is following the line of the ball.

CC, which may also be in the positions occupied by the dotted lines on either side of it, as its position varies with varying conditions, is supposed to mark the nearest points 3 can follow 2 and properly support him.

DD, also variable as above, is drawn to mark the nearest points 3 can effectively space ahead of 4.

Note.—CC and DD will vary according to the speed of the play and the length of strokes of the players holding the positions of 2, 3, and 4 and somewhat by the part of the field the play is in.

The area inclosed within the black lines indicates the most effective sphere of play for 3 and 2; either of these players outside of this area is out of place and can not and ordinarily will not be able to get into the play effectively. Neither player should ride out of this area unless accompanying the other, and even then it does not pay to follow an erring opponent too far. Where 2 rides right up onto 3 it is usually best for 3 to ride up with him, especially if 4 is ahead of his man.

Within this area the position to be taken by either player depends entirely upon the movements of the other. As it is only at the moment that the ball is struck at or ridden over that the player need watch the ball, it is safe to say that at least three-quarters of his time he must be watching his corresponding opponent and maneuvering to cover him, and less than one-quarter of his time should be spent watching the ball. Beginners always, and old players too often, concentrate their attention on the ball and let their opponents ride free, thus rendering their own play ineffective.

The dotted figures indicate the proper place for 3 to place himself when 2 is in other parts of the area.

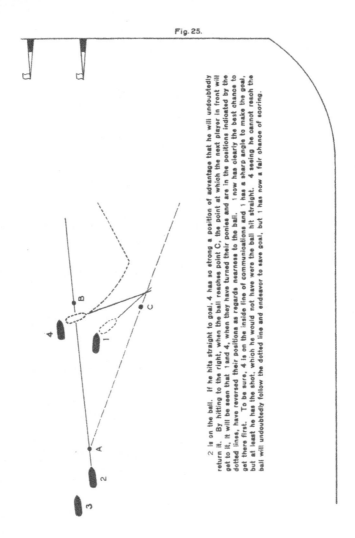

Fig. 25.

2 is on the ball. If he hits straight to goal, 4 has so strong a position of advantage that he will undoubtedly return it. By hitting to the right, when the ball reaches point C, the point at which the next player in front will get to it, it will be seen that 1 and 4, when they have turned their ponies and are in the positions indicated by the dotted lines, have reversed their positions as regards nearness to the ball. 1 now has clearly the best chance to get there first. To be sure, 4 is on the inside line of communications and 1 has a sharp angle to make the goal, but at least he has the shot, which he would not have were the ball hit straight. 4 seeing he cannot reach the ball will undoubtedly follow the dotted line and endeavor to save goal, but 1 has now a fair chance of scoring.

ACKNOWLEDGEMENTS

In putting together this edited and updated version of *As To Polo* I have had help and support from a number of wonderful members of the polo community. Ignacio Deltour reviewed and commented on the text and all diagrams and offered important feedback in language despite English being his second language. Erik Wright of Wrightway Polo and an instructor with the USPA was also helpful on form and content. Both Ignacio and Erik have added help to me in understanding some of the diagrams and descriptions as I was learning at the same time as I was editing. The staff at the Houghton Library at Harvard University offered assistance in searching archives for relevant data on Cam Forbes and his polo as well as Paul Elias from JM Forbes and Co who held the original copies published of *As To Polo*. Last but most certainly not least, thank you to Kali Browne (*https://about.me/kaliamanda*) who provided many hours of formatting, advice, and copy editing. I'm quite sure I could not have completed this project without her.

My sincere thanks to all of them.

Sukey Forbes

Made in the USA
Coppell, TX
17 August 2020